To my dearest friend,

I cannot count the times you have lifted my soul. Thank you so much for sharing so much of your life with me!

Your friend always,
with much love,

Sherry

POEMS THAT LIFT
THE SOUL

POEMS THAT LIFT THE SOUL

Edited by Jack M. Lyon, Linda Ririe Gundry, Jay A. Parry,
and Devan Jensen

SHADOW MOUNTAIN®

We acknowledge copyright holders whose material we may have included but with whom we were unable to make personal contact. Other works are in public domain. If any acknowledgments have been overlooked, please notify the publisher and omissions will be rectified in future editions.

Library of Congress Cataloging-in-Publication Data
Poems that lift the soul : a treasury of faith and inspiration /
    edited by Jack M. Lyon . . . [et al.].
        p.   cm.
    Includes indexes.
    ISBN 1-57345-364-1 (hb)
    1. Religious poetry, English. 2. Religious poetry, American.
I. Lyon, Jack M.
PR1191.P63   1998
821.008'0382—dc21   97-43382
                                                                     CIP

Printed in the United States of America   72082
10 9 8 7 6 5 4 3 2 1

CONTENTS

CONTENTS

PREFACE

"Poetry is the breath and finer spirit of all knowledge."
—WORDSWORTH

Poems That Lift the Soul was compiled in an effort to bring together in one place many favorite poems that touch the heart, inspire the mind, and soothe the spirit. It features quotable classics by past masters such as Shakespeare and Wordsworth and by relatively modern poets such as Ella Wheeler Wilcox and Edgar A. Guest. The poems are arranged by topic, with topics arranged alphabetically, and they are indexed by first line, author, and title.

The editors of this volume gratefully acknowledge permission to reproduce any poems that are not in the public domain. Every effort has been made to identify the authors of the poems and to obtain permission where necessary. We also express our appreciation to Ronald A. Millett, Sheri Dew, Patricia J. Parkinson, Jennifer Pritchett, and Ronald O. Stucki for their help in the publication of this volume.

ADVERSITY

WHAT GOD HATH PROMISED

God hath not promised
Skies always blue,
Flower-strewn pathways
All our lives through;
God hath not promised
Sun without rain,
Joy without sorrow,
Peace without pain.

But God hath promised
Strength for the day,
Rest for the labor,
Light for the way,
Grace for the trials,
Help from above,
Unfailing sympathy,
Undying love.

ANNIE JOHNSON FLINT

THE FEW

The easy roads are crowded
And the level roads are jammed;
The pleasant little rivers
With the drifting folks are crammed.
But off yonder where it's rocky,
Where you get a better view,
You will find the ranks are thinning
And the travelers are few.

Where the going's smooth and pleasant
You will always find the throng,
For the many, more's the pity,
Seem to like to drift along.

But the steeps that call for courage,
And the task that's hard to do,
In the end result in glory
For the never-wavering few.

EDGAR A. GUEST

ALONG THE ROAD

I walked a mile with Pleasure.
She chattered all the way,
But left me none the wiser
For all she had to say.

I walked a mile with Sorrow,
And ne'er a word said she;
But, oh, the things I learned from her
When Sorrow walked with me!

ROBERT BROWNING HAMILTON

ON HIS BLINDNESS

When I consider how my light is spent
   Ere half my days, in this dark world and wide,
   And that one talent, which is death to hide,
   Lodged with me useless, though my soul more bent
To serve therewith my Maker, and present
   My true account, lest he returning chide;
   "Doth God exact day-labor, light denied?"
   I fondly ask: But Patience, to prevent
That murmur, soon replies, "God doth not need
   Either man's work or his own gifts; who best
   Bear his mild yoke, they serve him best: his state
Is kingly; thousands at his bidding speed,
   And post o'er land and ocean without rest;
   They also serve who only stand and wait."

JOHN MILTON

FROM MILTON'S PRAYER FOR PATIENCE

I am old and blind!
Men point at me as smitten by God's frown:

2

Afflicted and deserted of my kind,
  Yet am I not cast down.

  I am weak, yet strong;
I murmur not that I no longer see;
Poor, old, and helpless, I the more belong,
  Father supreme, to thee!

  All-merciful One!
When men are furthest, then art Thou most near;
When friends pass by, my weaknesses to shun,
  Thy chariot I hear.

  Thy glorious face
Is leaning toward me; and its holy light
Shines in upon my lonely dwelling place,—
  And there is no more night.

  On my bended knee
I recognize thy purpose clearly shown:
My vision thou hast dimmed, that I may see
  Thyself, thyself alone.

Elizabeth Lloyd Howell

GETHSEMANE

  In golden youth when seems the earth
  A Summer-land of singing mirth,
  When souls are glad and hearts are light,
  And not a shadow lurks in sight,
  We do not know it, but there lies
  Somewhere veiled under evening skies
  A garden which we all must see—
  The garden of Gethsemane.

  With joyous steps we go our ways,
  Love lends a halo to our days;
  Light sorrows sail like clouds afar,
  We laugh, and say how strong we are.
  We hurry on; and hurrying, go
  Close to the border-land of woe
  That waits for you, and waits for me—
  For ever waits Gethsemane.

3

Down shadowy lanes, across strange streams,
Bridged over by our broken dreams;
Behind the misty caps of years,
Beyond the great salt fount of tears,
The garden lies. Strive as you may,
You cannot miss it in your way.
All paths that have been, or shall be,
Pass somewhere through Gethsemane.

All those who journey, soon or late,
Must pass within the garden's gate;
Must kneel alone in darkness there,
And battle with some fierce despair.
God pity those who cannot say,
"Not mine but thine," who only pray,
"Let this cup pass," and cannot see
The *purpose* in Gethsemane.

ELLA WHEELER WILCOX

THE LOOM OF TIME

Man's life is laid in the loom of time
    To a pattern he does not see,
While the weavers work and the shuttles fly
    Till the dawn of eternity.

Some shuttles are filled with silver threads
    And some with threads of gold,
While often but the darker hues
    Are all that they may hold.

But the weaver watches with skillful eye
    Each shuttle fly to and fro,
And sees the pattern so deftly wrought
    As the loom moves sure and slow.

God surely planned the pattern:
    Each thread, the dark and fair,
Is chosen by His master skill
    And placed in the web with care.

4

He only knows its beauty,
　　And guides the shuttles which hold
The threads so unattractive,
　　As well as the threads of gold.

Not till each loom is silent
　　And the shuttles cease to fly
Shall God reveal the pattern
　　And explain the reason why

The dark threads were as needful
　　In the weaver's skillful hand
As the threads of gold and silver
　　For the pattern which He planned.

AUTHOR UNKNOWN

THO LOSSES AND CROSSES

Tho losses and crosses be lessons right severe,
There's wit there ye'll get there
　　You'll find no other where.

ROBERT BURNS

ANSWER TO PRAYER

We ask for strength and God gives us
　　difficulties which make us strong.
We pray for wisdom and God sends us problems,
　　the solution of which develops wisdom.
We plead for prosperity and God gives us
　　brain and brawn to work.
We plead for courage and God gives us
　　dangers to overcome.
We ask for favors—God gives us opportunities.
—This is the answer.

AUTHOR UNKNOWN

GOD BROKE OUR YEARS TO HOURS AND DAYS

God broke our years to hours and days,
　　That hour by hour and day by day,

Just going on a little way,
We might be able all along to keep quite strong.
   Should all the weight of life
Be laid across our shoulders, and the future, rife
With woe and struggle, meet us face to face
      At just one place,
      We could not go;
      Our feet would stop; and so
God lays a little on us every day,
And never, I believe, on all the way
      Will burdens bear so deep
Or pathways lie so threatening and so steep
   But we can go, if by God's power
   We only bear the burden of the hour.

GEORGE KLINGLE

THE RAINY DAY

The day is cold and dark and dreary;
It rains, and the wind is never weary;
The vine still clings to the moldering wall,
But at every gust the dead leaves fall,
   And the day is dark and dreary.

My life is cold and dark and dreary;
It rains, and the wind is never weary;
My thoughts still cling to the moldering past,
But the hopes of youth fall thick in the blast,
   And the days are dark and dreary.

Be still, sad heart! and cease repining;
Behind the clouds is the sun still shining:
Thy fate is the common fate of all:
Into each life some rain must fall,
   Some days must be dark and dreary.

HENRY WADSWORTH LONGFELLOW

HE SENDETH SUN

He sendeth sun; he sendeth shower;
Alike they're needful to the flower;

6

And joys and tears alike are sent
To give the soul fit nourishment.
As comes to me or cloud or sun
Father, thy will, not mine, be done.

SARAH FLOWER ADAMS

FROM ROOFS

They say that life is a highway,
    And its milestones are the years;
And now and then there's a toll gate,
    Where you buy your way with your tears.

It's a rough road and a steep road,
    And it stretches broad and far,
But at last it leads to a golden town
    Where the golden houses are.

JOYCE KILMER

WORTH WHILE

It is easy enough to be pleasant
When life flows by like a song,
But the man worth while is one who will smile
When everything goes dead wrong.
For the test of the heart is trouble,
And it always comes with the years,
And the smile that is worth the praises of earth
Is the smile that shines through tears.

It is easy enough to be prudent,
When nothing tempts you to stray,
When without or within no voice of sin
Is luring your soul away;
But it's only a negative virtue
Until it is tried by fire,
And the life that is worth the honor of earth
Is the one that resists desire.

By the cynic, the sad, the fallen,
Who had no strength for the strife,

7

The world's highway is cumbered to-day;
They make up the sum of life.
But the virtue that conquers passion,
And the sorrow that hides in a smile,
It is these that are worth the homage of earth,
For we find them but once in a while.

ELLA WHEELER WILCOX

ADVERSITY

Sweet are the uses of adversity,
Which, like the toad, ugly and venomous,
Wears yet a precious jewel in his head.

WILLIAM SHAKESPEARE, *AS YOU LIKE IT* 2.1.12–14

Additional poems about adversity appear in the topics "Character,"
"Courage," "Death and Immortality," "Perseverance," and elsewhere.

AGING

FROM RABBI BEN EZRA

Grow old along with me!
The best is yet to be,
The last of life, for which the first was made:
Our times are in His hand,
Who saith "A whole I planned,
Youth shows but half; trust God; see all, nor be afraid!"

ROBERT BROWNING

AS I GROW OLD

God keep my heart attuned to laughter
When youth is done;
When all the days are gray days, coming after
The warmth, the sun.
God keep me then from bitterness, from grieving,
When life seems cold;
God keep me always loving and believing
As I grow old.

AUTHOR UNKNOWN

HOW OLD ARE YOU?

Age is a quality of the mind.
If you have left your dreams behind,
If hope is cold,
If you no longer look ahead,
If your ambitions' fires are dead—
Then you are old.

But if from life you take the best,
If in life you keep the jest,
If love you hold;
No matter how the years go by,
No matter how the birthdays fly—
You are not old.

H. S. FRITSCH

9

BLISS

There's a bliss beyond all that the minstrel has told,
When two, that are link'd in one heavenly tie,
With heart never changing, and brow never cold,
Love on through all ills, and love on till they die.
One hour of a passion so sacred is worth
Whole ages of heartless and wandering bliss;
And oh! if there be [any heaven] on earth,
It is this—it is this!

THOMAS MOORE

A LITTLE MORE TIRED

A little more tired at close of day,
A little less anxious to have our way;
A little less ready to scold and blame,
A little more care of a brother's name;
And so we are nearing our journey's end,
Where time and eternity meet and blend.

ROLLIN JOHN WELLS

FROM MEN TOLD ME, LORD!

Men told me, Lord, it was a vale of tears
Where thou hadst placed me; wickedness and woe
My twain companions whereso I might go;
That I through ten and three-score weary years
Should stumble on, beset by pains and fears. . . .
When all was ended then I should demand
Full compensation from thine austere hand:
For 'tis thy pleasure, all temptation past,
To be not just but generous at last.
Lord, here am I, my three-score years and ten
Are counted to the full; I've fought thy fight,
Crossed thy dark valleys, scaled thy rocks' harsh height,
Borne all the burdens thou dost lay on men
With hand unsparing, three-score years and ten.
Before thee now I make my claim, Oh, Lord!
What shall I pay thee as a meet reward?

DAVID STARR JORDAN

THE FLIGHT OF YOUTH

There are gains for all our losses.
    There are balms for all our pain:
But when youth, the dream, departs
It takes something from our hearts,
    And it never comes again.

We are stronger, and are better,
    Under manhood's sterner reign:
Still we feel that something sweet
Followed youth, with flying feet,
    And will never come again.

Something beautiful is vanished,
    And we sigh for it in vain;
We behold it everywhere,
On the earth, and in the air,
    But it never comes again!

RICHARD HENRY STODDARD

WHEN I AM OLD

When I am old—and O, how soon
Will life's sweet morning yield to noon,
And noon's broad, fervid, earnest light
Be shaded in the solemn night,
Till, like a story well-nigh told,
Will seem my life—when I am old.

When I am old, this breezy earth
Will lose for me its voice of mirth;
The streams will have an undertone
Of sadness not by right their own;
And Spring's sweet power in vain unfold
In rosy charms—when I am old.

When I am old, I shall not care
To deck with flowers my faded hair;
'Twill be no vain desire of mine
In rich and costly dress to shine;
Bright jewels and the brightest gold
Will charm me naught—when I am old.

11

When I am old, my friends will be
Old and infirm and bowed like me;
Or else (their bodies 'neath the sod,
Their spirits dwelling safe with God),
The old church bells will long have tolled
Above the rest—when I am old.

When I am old, I'd rather bend
Thus sadly o'er each buried friend
Than see them lose the earnest truth
That marks the friendship of our youth;
'Twill be so sad to have them cold
Or strange to me—when I am old!

When I am old—O! how it seems
Like the wild lunacy of dreams
To picture in prophetic rhyme
That dim, far-distant, shadowy time—
So distant that it seems o'erbold
Even to say, "When I am old."

Ere I am old—that time is now;
For youth sits lightly on my brow;
My limbs are firm, and strong, and free;
Life hath a thousand charms for me—
Charms that will long their influence hold
Within my heart—ere I am old.

Ere I am old, O! let me give
My life to learning how to live;
Then shall I meet, with willing heart,
An early summons to depart,
Or find my lengthened days consoled
By God's sweet peace—when I am old.

CAROLINE ATHERTON MASON

OLD AGE

The seas are quiet when the winds give o'er;
So calm are we when passions are no more.
For then we know how vain it was to boast
Of fleeting things, so certain to be lost.

12

Clouds of affection from our younger eyes
Conceal that emptiness which age descries.

The soul's dark cottage, battered and decayed,
Lets in new light through chinks that Time hath made:
Stronger by weakness, wiser men become
As they draw near to their eternal home.
Leaving the old, both worlds at once they view
That stand upon the threshold of the new.

EDMUND WALLER

Additional poems about aging appear in the topics "Adversity," "Death and Immortality," "Life," and elsewhere.

CHARACTER

SOW A THOUGHT

Sow a thought, reap an act;
Sow an act, reap a habit;
Sow a habit, reap a character;
Sow a character, reap an eternal destiny.

E. D. BOARDMAN

BE STRONG!

Be strong!
We are not here to play, to dream, to drift,
We have hard work to do, and loads to lift.
Shun not the struggle, face it, 'tis God's gift.

Be strong!
Say not the days are evil—who's to blame!
And fold the hands and acquiesce—O shame!
Stand up, speak out, and bravely, in God's name.

Be strong!
It matters not how deep entrenched the wrong,
How hard the battle goes, the day, how long;
Faint not, fight on! To-morrow comes the song.

MALTBIE D. BABCOCK

GIVE US MEN!

Give us Men!
Men—from every rank,
Fresh and free and frank;
Men of thought and reading,
Men of light and leading,
Men of loyal breeding,
The nation's welfare speeding;
Men of faith and not of fiction,

Men of lofty aim in action;
   Give us Men—I say again,
      Give us Men!

Give us Men!
Strong and stalwart ones;
Men whom highest hope inspires,
Men whom purest honor fires,
Men who trample self beneath them,
Men who make their country wreathe them
   As her noble sons,
      Worthy of their sires;
Men who never shame their mothers,
Men who never fail their brothers,
True, however false are others:
   Give us Men—I say again,
      Give us Men!

Give us Men!
Men who, when the tempest gathers,
Grasp the standard of their fathers
   In the thickest fight;
Men who strike for home and altar,
(Let the coward cringe and falter),
   God defend the right!
True as truth the lorn and lonely,
Tender, as the brave are only;
Men who tread where saints have trod,
Men for Country, Home—and God:
   Give us Men! I say again—again—
      Give us Men!

JOSIAH GILBERT HOLLAND

LORD, GIVE ME NOT JUST WORDS TO SAY

Lord, give me not just words to say,
   Tho' I need right words too,
But strength to live in such a way
   My life will make my words come true.

AUTHOR UNKNOWN

A LIFE HEROIC

I like the man who faces what he must
   With step triumphant and a heart of cheer;
   Who fights the daily battle without fear;
Sees his hopes fail, yet keeps unfaltering trust
That God is God; that somehow, true and just
   His plans work out for mortals; not a tear
   Is shed when fortune, which the world holds dear,
Falls from his grasp; better, with love, a crust
Than living in dishonor; envies not
   Nor loses faith in man; but does his best
Nor ever mourns over his humbler lot,
   But with a smile and words of hope, gives zest
To every toiler; he alone is great
Who by a life heroic conquers fate.

SARAH K. BOLTON

HE THAT HAS LIGHT

He that has light within his own clear breast
May sit i' the centre, and enjoy bright day:
But he that hides a dark soul and foul thoughts,
Benighted walks under the mid-day sun;
Himself in his own dungeon.

JOHN MILTON

FOR THOSE WHO FAIL

"All honor to him who shall win the prize,"
   The world has cried for a thousand years;
But to him who tries and who fails and dies,
   I give great honor and glory and tears.

O great is the hero who wins a name,
   But greater many and many a time,
Some pale-faced fellow who dies in shame,
   And lets God finish the thought sublime.

16

And great is the man with the sword undrawn,
  And good is the man who refrains from wine;
But the man who fails and yet fights on,
  Lo! he is the twin-born brother of mine!

JOAQUIN MILLER

FROM JULIUS CAESAR

His life was gentle, and the elements
So mix'd in him that Nature might stand up
And say to all the world "This was a man!"

WILLIAM SHAKESPEARE, JULIUS CAESAR 5.5.73–75

WE ARE BUILDING EVERY DAY

We are building every day,
In a good or evil way;
And the building, as it grows,
Shall our inmost selves disclose,
And, in every arch and line,
All our faults and failings find.

We may build a palace grand,
Or a wreck upon the sand.
Do you ask what building this,
That can show both pain and bliss,
That can be both dark and fair?
Lo, its name is Character.

Build it well what'er you do,
Build it straight and strong and true.
Build it clean, and high, and broad,
Build it for the eyes of God.

AUTHOR UNKNOWN

WILL

There is no chance, no destiny, no fate,
  Can circumvent or hinder or control
  The firm resolve of a determined soul.
Gifts count for nothing; will alone is great;
All things give way before it, soon or late.

What obstacle can stay the mighty force
Of the sea-seeking river in its course,
Or cause the ascending orb of day to wait?

Each wellborn soul must win what it deserves.
Let the fool prate of luck. The fortunate
Is he whose earnest purpose never swerves,
Whose slightest action or inaction serves
The one great aim. Why, even Death stands still,
And waits an hour sometimes for such a will.

ELLA WHEELER WILCOX

YOU TELL ON YOURSELF

You tell on yourself by the friends you seek,
By the very manner in which you speak,
By the way you employ your leisure time,
By the use you make of dollar and dime.
You tell what you are by the things you wear,
And even by the way you wear your hair,
By the kind of things at which you laugh,
By the records you play on your phonograph.
You tell what you are by the way you walk,
By the things of which you delight to talk,
By the manner in which you bury deceit,
By so simple a thing as how you eat.
By the books you choose from the well-filled shelf.
In these ways and more you tell on yourself.

AUTHOR UNKNOWN

Additional poems about character appear in the topics "Courage," "Divine Nature," "Integrity," and elsewhere.

CHILDREN

NOBODY KNOWS WHAT A BOY IS WORTH

Nobody knows what a boy is worth,
We'll have to wait and see.
But every man in a noble place
A boy once used to be.

AUTHOR UNKNOWN

CHILD'S EVENING HYMN

Now the day is over,
    Night is drawing nigh,
Shadows of the evening
    Steal across the sky.

Now the darkness gathers,
    Stars begin to peep,
Birds and beasts and flowers
    Soon will be asleep.

Jesus, give the weary
    Calm and sweet repose,
With thy tenderest blessing
    May our eyelids close.

Grant to little children
    Visions bright of thee,
Guard the sailors tossing
    On the deep blue sea.

Comfort every sufferer
    Watching late in pain;
Those who plan some evil
    From their sin restrain.

Through the long night-watches
    May thy angels keep
Loving watch about me,
    Guarding as I sleep.

When the morning wakens,
    Then may I arise
Pure and fresh and sinless
    In thy holy eyes.

SABINE BARING-GOULD, ADAPTED

WHO TOUCHES A BOY BY THE MASTER'S PLAN

Who touches a boy by the Master's plan
Is shaping the course of a future man,
Is dealing with one who is living seed
And may be a man whom the world will need.

AUTHOR UNKNOWN

FROM THE CHILDREN

When daily chores all are ended,
And playtime for day is dismissed,
And the little ones gather around me
To say good-night prayers and be kissed,
Oh! the little white arms that encircle
My neck in a tender embrace!
Oh! the smiles that are haloes of Heaven
Shed sunshine of joy on my face!

When they're in their beds, I sit dreaming
Of my childhood, too lovely to last;
Of love that my heart well remembers
When it wakes to the pulse of the past
'Fore I noticed the mean things around me,
Unaware of sorrow and sin—
Then, the glory of God was about me,
And the glory of gladness within.

Oh! my heart goes back to my children
And my thoughts and feelings flow
As I think of the path, steep and stony,
Where the feet of my dear ones must go;
Of the mountains of sin hanging o'er them,
Of the tempest of fate flowing wild;
Oh! there's nothing on earth half so holy
As the innocent heart of a child.

They are idols of hearts and of household!
They are angels of God in disguise;
The sunlight still sleeps in their tresses,
His glory still gleams in their eyes;
These truants from home and from Heaven,
They have made me more gentle and mild;
And I know now how Jesus could liken
The kingdom of God to a child.

CHARLES M. DICKINSON

A PARENTAL ODE TO MY SON
AGED THREE YEARS AND FIVE MONTHS

Thou happy, happy elf!
(But stop,—first let me kiss away that tear!)
Thou tiny image of myself!
(My love, he's poking peas into his ear!)
Thou merry, laughing sprite,
With spirits feather-light,
Untouched by sorrow, and unsoiled by sin,—
(My dear, the child is swallowing a pin!)

Thou little tricksy Puck!
With antics toys so funnily bestuck,
Light as the singing bird that wings the air,—
(The door! the door! he'll tumble down the stair!)
Thou darling of thy sire!
(Why, Jane, he'll set his pinafore afire!)
Thou imp of mirth and joy!
In Love's dear chain so strong and bright a link,
Thou idol of thy parents,—(Drat the boy!
There goes my ink!)

* * *

Thou enviable being!
No storms, no clouds, in thy blue sky foreseeing,
Play on, play on,
My elfin John!
Toss the light ball, bestride the stick,—
(I knew so many cakes would make him sick!)
With fancies, buoyant as the thistle-down,
Prompting the face grotesque, and antic brisk,
With many a lamb-like frisk!
(He's got the scissors, snipping at your gown!)

21

Thou pretty opening rose!
(Go to your mother, child, and wipe your nose!)
Balmy and breathing music like the South,—
(He really brings my heart into my mouth!)
Fresh as the morn, and brilliant as its star,—
(I wish that window had an iron bar!)
Bold as the hawk, yet gentle as the dove;—
(I'll tell you what, my love,
I cannot write unless he's sent above.)

THOMAS HOOD

THE CHILDREN'S HOUR

Between the dark and the daylight,
    When the night is beginning to lower,
Comes a pause in the day's occupations
    That is known as the Children's Hour.

I hear in the chamber above me
    The patter of little feet,
The sound of a door that is opened,
    And voices soft and sweet.

From my study I see in the lamplight,
    Descending the broad hall stair,
Grave Alice, and laughing Allegra,
    And Edith with golden hair.

A whisper, and then a silence:
    Yet I know by their merry eyes
They are plotting and planning together
    To take me by surprise.

A sudden rush from the stairway,
    A sudden raid from the hall!
By three doors left unguarded
    They enter my castle wall!

They climb up into my turret
    O'er the arms and back of my chair;
If I try to escape, they surround me;
    They seem to be everywhere.

They almost devour me with kisses,
    Their arms about me entwine,
Till I think of the Bishop of Bingen
    In his Mouse-Tower on the Rhine!

Do you think, O blue-eyed banditti,
    Because you have scaled the wall,
Such an old mustachio as I am
    Is not a match for you all!

I have you fast in my fortress,
    And will not let you depart,
But put you down into the dungeon
    In the round-tower of my heart.

And there will I keep you forever,
    Yes, forever and a day,
Till the walls shall crumble to ruin,
    And moulder in dust away.

HENRY WADSWORTH LONGFELLOW

THERE WAS A CHILD WENT FORTH

There was a child went forth every day,
And the first object he look'd upon, that object he became,
Men and women crowding fast in the streets, if they are not flashes and specks what are they?
The streets themselves and the facades of houses, and goods in the windows,
Vehicles, teams, the heavy-plank'd wharves, the huge crossing at the ferries,
The village on the highland seen from afar at sunset, the river between,
Shadows, aureola and mist, the light falling on roofs and gables of white or brown two miles off,
The schooner near by sleepily dropping down the tide, the little boat slack-tow'd astern,
The hurrying tumbling waves, quick-broken crests, slapping,
The strata of color'd clouds, the long bar of maroon-tint away solitary by itself, the spread of purity it lies motionless in,

The horizon's edge, the flying sea-crow, the fragrance of salt marsh
    and shore mud,
These became part of that child who went forth every day, and who
    now goes, and will always go forth every day.

WALT WHITMAN

THE SCULPTOR MAY CHIP THE MARBLE BLOCK

The sculptor may chip the marble block,
The painter a blot erase,
But the teacher who wounds a little child
May never his fault efface.

O realize then, indifferent one,
In moulding a plastic soul
The blight you cause, the scar you make
May meet you at Judgment's roll.

AUTHOR UNKNOWN

TWO AND A HALF

Hold him a little longer,
Rock him a little more.
Tell him another story
(You've only told him four).
Let him sleep on your shoulder,
Rejoice in his happy smile.
He is only two and a half
For such a little while!

AUTHOR UNKNOWN

*Additional poems about children appear in the topics "Fatherhood," "Home
and Family," "Motherhood," and elsewhere.*

CHOICE AND ACCOUNTABILITY

A BAG OF TOOLS

Isn't it strange that princes and kings
    And clowns that caper in sawdust rings
And just plain folks like you and me
    Are builders for eternity?

To each is given a bag of tools,
    A shapeless mass and a book of rules,
And each must build, ere life has flown,
    A stumbling block or a steppingstone.

R. L. SHARPE

IT SHOWS IN YOUR FACE

You don't have to tell how you live each day,
You don't have to say if you work or play,
A tried, true barometer serves in your place;
However you live, it will show in your face.
The false, the deceit that you bear in your heart
Will not stay inside, where it first got a start,
For sinew and blood are a thin veil of lace;
What you wear in your heart you wear in your face.
If your life is unselfish, if for others you live
For not what you get, but for what you can give,
If you live close to God, in His infinite grace,
You don't have to tell it; it shows in your face.

AUTHOR UNKNOWN

A NAME IN THE SAND

Alone I walked the ocean strand,
    A pearly shell was in my hand;
I stooped and wrote upon the sand
    My name, the year, the day;
As onward from the spot I passed,
One lingering look behind I cast,

A wave came rolling high and fast
   And washed my lines away.

And so, I thought, 'twill quickly be
With every mark on earth from me;
A wave of dark oblivion's sea
   Will sweep across the place
Where I have trod the sandy shore
Of time, and been, to be no more,—
Of me, my day, the name I bore,
   To leave no track nor trace.

And yet, with Him who counts the sands,
And holds the waters in his hands,
I know a lasting record stands
   Inscribed against my name,
Of all this mortal part has wrought,
Of all this thinking soul has thought,
All, from these fleeting moments caught,
   For glory or for shame.

GEORGE DENISON PRENTICE

FROM JUSTICE

We get back our mete as we measure,
   We cannot do wrong and feel right,
Nor can we give pain and feel pleasure,
   For justice avenges each slight.

ALICE CARY

MAN-TEST

When in the dim beginning of the years,
God mixed in man the raptures and the tears
And scattered through his brain the starry stuff,
He said, "Behold! Yet this is not enough,
For I must test his spirit to make sure
That he can dare the Vision and endure.

"I will withdraw my Face,
Veil me in shadow for a certain space,

Leaving behind Me only a broken clue—
A crevice where the glory shimmers through,
Some whisper from the sky,
Some footprints in the road to track Me by.

"I will leave man to make the fateful guess,
Will leave him torn between the No and Yes,
Leave him unresting till he rests in Me,
Drawn upward by the choice that makes him free—
Leave him in tragic loneliness to choose,
With all in life to win or all to lose."

EDWIN MARKHAM

THE WAYS

To every man there openeth
A Way, and Ways, and a Way.
And the High Soul climbs the High Way,
And the Low Soul gropes the Low,
And in between, on the misty flats,
The rest drift to and fro.
But to every man there openeth
A High Way, and a Low.
And every man decideth
The Way his soul shall go.

JOHN OXENHAM

MR. MEANT-TO

Mr. Meant-to has a comrade,
And his name is Didn't-do.
Have you ever chanced to meet them?
Did they ever call on you?

These two fellows live together
In the house of Never-win,
And I'm told that it is haunted
By the ghost of Might-have-been.

AUTHOR UNKNOWN

27

BUILDING FOR ETERNITY

We are building in sorrow or joy
A temple the world may not see,
Which time cannot mar nor destroy;
We build for eternity.

We are building ev'ry day,
A temple the world may not see;
Building, building ev'ry day,
Building for eternity.

Ev'ry thought that we've ever had
Its own little place has filled;
Ev'ry deed we have done, good or bad,
Is a stone in the temple we build.

Ev'ry word that so lightly falls,
Giving some heart joy or pain,
Will shine in our temple walls,
Or ever its beauty stain.

Are you building for God alone—
Are you building in faith and love
A temple the Father will own
In the city of light above?

N. B. Sargent

KNOW THIS, THAT EVERY SOUL IS FREE

Know this, that ev'ry soul is free
To choose his life and what he'll be;
For this eternal truth is giv'n:
That God will force no man to heav'n.

He'll call, persuade, direct aright,
And bless with wisdom, love, and light,
In nameless ways be good and kind,
But never force the human mind.

Freedom and reason make us men;
Take these away, what are we then?

Mere animals, and just as well
The beasts may think of heav'n or hell.

May we no more our pow'rs abuse,
But ways of truth and goodness choose;
Our God is pleased when we improve
His grace and seek his perfect love.

AUTHOR UNKNOWN

THE ROAD NOT TAKEN

Two roads diverged in a yellow wood,
And sorry I could not travel both
And be one traveler, long I stood
And looked down one as far as I could
To where it bent in the undergrowth;

Then took the other, as just as fair,
And having perhaps the better claim,
Because it was grassy and wanted wear;
Though as for that the passing there
Had worn them really about the same,

And both that morning equally lay
In leaves no step had trodden black.
Oh, I kept the first for another day!
Yet knowing how way leads on to way,
I doubted if I should ever come back.

I shall be telling this with a sigh
Somewhere ages and ages hence:
Two roads diverged in a wood, and I—
I took the one less traveled by,
And that has made all the difference.

ROBERT FROST

Additional poems about choice and accountability appear in the topics "Character," "Self-Mastery," and elsewhere.

CHRISTMAS

CHRISTMAS EVERYWHERE

Everywhere, everywhere, Christmas tonight!
Christmas in lands of the fir-tree and pine,
Christmas in lands of the palm-tree and vine,
Christmas where snow peaks stand solemn and white,
Christmas where cornfields stand sunny and bright.
Christmas where children are hopeful and gay,
Christmas where old men are patient and gray,
Christmas where peace, like a dove in his flight,
Broods o'er brave men in the thick of the fight;
Everywhere, everywhere, Christmas tonight!
For the Christ-child who comes is the Master of all;
No palace too great, no cottage too small.

PHILLIPS BROOKS

BRIGHTEST AND BEST OF THE SONS OF THE MORNING

Brightest and best of the sons of the morning
Dawn on our darkness and lend us thine aid;
Star of the east, the horizon adorning,
Guide where our infant Redeemer is laid.

Cold on His cradle the dew drops are shining,
Low lies His head with the beasts of the stall;
Angels adore Him in slumber reclining.
Maker, and Monarch, and Savior of all.

Say, shall we yield Him, in costly devotion,
Odors of Edom, and offerings divine?
Gems of the mountain and pearls of the ocean,
Myrrh from the forest or gold from the mine?

Vainly we offer each ample oblation;
Vainly with gifts would His favor secure,
Richer by far is the heart's adoration;
Dearer to God are the prayers of the poor.

A. C. SMYTH

LIGHT OF THE WORLD

Light of the world so clear and bright,
Enter our homes this Christmas night;
Relight our souls so tenderly,
That we may grow to be like Thee.

AUTHOR UNKNOWN

CHRISTMAS LEGENDS

Christmas morn, the legends say,
Even the cattle kneel to pray,
Even the beasts of wood and field
Homage to Christ the Saviour yield.
Horse and cow and woolly sheep
Wake themselves from their heavy sleep,
Bending heads and knees to Him
Who came to earth in a stable dim.
Far away in the forest dark
Creatures timidly wake and hark,
Feathered bird and furry beast
Turn their eyes to the mystic East.
Loud at the dawning, chanticleer
Sounds his note, the rest of the year,
But Christmas Eve the whole night long
Honouring Christ he sings his song.
Christmas morn, the legends say,
Even the cattle kneel to pray,
Even the wildest beast afar
Knows the light of the Saviour's star.

DENIS A. MCCARTHY

A HYMN ON THE NATIVITY OF MY SAVIOUR

I sing the birth was born tonight,
The author both of life and light;
    The angels so did sound it.
And like the ravished shepherds said,
Who saw the light and were afraid,
    Yet searched, and true they found it.

BEN JONSON

31

ALL ARE VOCAL WITH HIS NAME

The silent skies are full of speech
　　For who hath ears to hear;
The winds are whispering each to each,
The moon is calling to the beach,
And stars their sacred wisdom teach
　　Of faith and love and fear.

But once the sky the silence broke
　　And song o'erflowed the earth;
The midnight air with glory shook,
And angels mortal language spoke,
When God our human nature took
　　In Christ, the Savior's birth.

And Christmas once is Christmas still;
　　The gates through which he came,
And forests' wild and murmuring rill,
And fruitful field and breezy hill,
And all that else the wide world fill
　　Are vocal with his name.

Shall we not listen while they sing
　　This latest Christmas morn;
And music hear in everything,
And faithful lives in tribute bring
To the great song which greets the King,
　　Who comes when Christ is born?

PHILLIPS BROOKS

THE CHRISTMAS SYMBOL

Only a manger, cold and bare,
　　Only a maiden mild,
Only some shepherds kneeling there,
　　Watching a little Child;
And yet that maiden's arms enfold
　　The King of Heaven above;
And in the Christ-Child we behold
　　The Lord of Life and Love.

AUTHOR UNKNOWN

32

ON THE MORNING OF CHRIST'S NATIVITY

I

This is the month, and this the happy morn,
Wherein the Son of Heaven's eternal King,
Of wedded Maid and Virgin Mother born,
Our great redemption from above did bring;
For so the holy sages once did sing,
    That he our deadly forfeit should release,
And with his Father work us a perpetual peace.

II

That glorious form, that light unsufferable,
And that far-beaming blaze of majesty,
Wherewith he wont at Heaven's high council-table
To sit the midst of Trinal Unity,
He laid aside; and here with us to be,
    Forsook the courts of everlasting day,
And chose with us a darksome house of mortal clay. . . .

V

But peaceful was the night
Wherein the Prince of Light
    His reign of peace upon the earth began:
The winds with wonder whist,
Smoothly the waters kissed,
    Whispering new joys to the mild ocean,
Who now hath quite forgot to rave,
While birds of calm sit brooding on the charmed wave.

VI

The stars with deep amaze
Stand fixed in steadfast gaze,
    Bending one way their precious influence,
And will not take their flight
For all the morning light,
    Or Lucifer that often warned them thence;
But in their glimmering orbs did glow,
Until their Lord himself bespake, and bid them go.

JOHN MILTON

AT CHRISTMAS BE MERRY

At Christmas be merry, and thankful withal,
And feast thy poor neighbours, the great with the small.

THOMAS TUSSER

A CHRISTMAS HYMN

Love came down at Christmas,
Love all lovely, Love Divine;
Love was born at Christmas,
Star and Angels gave the sign.

* * *

Love shall be our token,
Love be yours and love be mine,
Love to God and all men,
Love for plea and gift and sign.

CHRISTINA ROSSETTI

PRAYER ON CHRISTMAS EVE

O wondrous night of star and song,
  O blessed Christmas night!
Lord, make me feel my whole life long
  Its loveliness and light!
So all the years my heart shall thrill
Remembering angels on a hill,
And one lone star shall bless me still
  On every Christmas night!

NANCY BYRD TURNER

THERE'S A SONG IN THE AIR!

There's a song in the air!
There's a star in the sky!
There's a mother's deep prayer
And a baby's low cry!
And the star rains its fire while the beautiful sing,
For the manger of Bethlehem cradles a King!

There's a tumult of joy
O'er the wonderful birth,
For the Virgin's sweet boy
Is the Lord of the earth.
Ay! the star rains its fire while the beautiful sing,
For the manger of Bethlehem cradles a King!

In the light of that star
Lie the ages impearled;
And that song from afar
Has swept over the world.
Every hearth is aflame, and the beautiful sing
In the homes of the nations that Jesus is King!

We rejoice in the light,
And we echo the song
That comes down thro' the night
From the heavenly throng.
Ay! we shout to the lovely evangel they bring,
And we greet in His cradle our Saviour and King!

JOSIAH GILBERT HOLLAND

MY GIFT

Nor crown, nor robe, nor spice I bring
As offering unto Christ, my King.
Yet have I brought a gift the Child
May not despise, however small;
For here I lay my heart today,
And it is full of love to all.
Take Thou the poor but loyal thing,
My only tribute, Christ, my King!

EUGENE FIELD

THE THREE KINGS

Three Kings came riding from far away,
    Melchior and Gaspar and Baltasar;
Three Wise Men out of the East were they,
And they travelled by night and they slept by day,
    For their guide was a beautiful, wonderful star.

35

The star was so beautiful, large, and clear,
    That all the other stars of the sky
Became a white mist in the atmosphere,
And by this they knew that the coming was near
    Of the Prince foretold in the prophecy.

Three caskets they bore on their saddlebows,
    Three caskets of gold with golden keys;
Their robes were of crimson silk with rows
Of bells and pomegranates and furbelows,
    Their turbans like blossoming almond-trees.

And so the Three Kings rode into the West,
    Through the dusk of night, over hill and dell,
And sometimes they nodded with beard on breast,
And sometimes talked, as they paused to rest,
    With the people they met at some wayside well.

"Of the child that is born," said Baltasar,
    "Good people, I pray you, tell us the news;
For we in the East have seen his star,
And have ridden fast, and have ridden far,
    To find and worship the King of the Jews."

And the people answered, "You ask in vain;
    We know of no king but Herod the Great!"
They thought the Wise Men were men insane,
As they spurred their horses across the plain,
    Like riders in haste, and who cannot wait.

And when they came to Jerusalem,
    Herod, the Great, who had heard this thing,
Sent for the Wise Men and questioned them;
And said, "Go down unto Bethlehem,
    And bring me tidings of this new king."

So they rode away; and the star stood still,
    The only one in the gray of morn;
Yes, it stopped,—it stood still of its own free will,
Right over Bethlehem on the hill,
    The city of David, where Christ was born.

And the Three Kings rode through the gate and the guard,
    Through the silent street, till their horses turned
And neighed as they entered the great inn yard;
But the windows were closed, and the doors were barred,
    And only a light in the stable burned.

And cradled there in the scented hay,
    In the air made sweet by the breath of kine,
The little child in the manger lay,
The child, that would be king one day
    Of a kingdom not human but divine.

His mother Mary of Nazareth
    Sat watching beside his place of rest,
Watching the even flow of his breath,
For the joy of life and the terror of death
    Were mingled together in her breast.

They laid their offerings at his feet:
    The gold was their tribute to a King,
The frankincense, with its odor sweet,
Was for the Priest, the Paraclete,
    The myrrh for the body's burying.

And the mother wondered and bowed her head,
    And sat as still as a statue of stone;
Her heart was troubled yet comforted,
Remembering what the Angel had said
    Of an endless reign and of David's throne.

Then the Kings rode out of the city gate,
    With a clatter of hoofs in proud array;
But they went not back to Herod the Great,
For they knew his malice and feared his hate,
    And returned to their homes by another way.

HENRY WADSWORTH LONGFELLOW

A CHRISTMAS CAROL

Before the paling of the stars,
    Before the winter morn,
Before the earliest cock-crow

Jesus Christ was born:
Born in a stable,
Cradled in a manger,
In the world His hands had made
Born a stranger. . . .

Jesus on His mother's breast
In the stable cold,
Spotless Lamb of God was He,
Shepherd of the fold:
Let us kneel with Mary maid,
With Joseph bent and hoary,
With saint and angel, ox and ass,
To hail the King of Glory.

CHRISTINA ROSSETTI

GIFTS OF THE FIRST CHRISTMAS

Adorned with carven gems and gold
The sages bore from eastern lands
Gifts for the tiny new-come King.
Came He with empty hands?—

Stronger than frankincense and myrrh,
There followed Him across the dark
The dawn-clean breath of better life
To fan the immortal spark.

And the stars greyed in the slow dawn;
The shimmer of the gold grew dim
Beside the deep far-shining light
That poured for Him.

CARLTON CULMSEE

THE EARTH HAS GROWN OLD

The Earth has grown old with its burden of care
But at Christmas it always is young;
The heart of the jewel burns lustrous and fair,
And its soul, full of music, breaks forth on the air
When the song of the angels is sung.

It is coming, Old Earth, it is coming tonight!
    On the snowflakes which cover thy sod
The feet of the Christ-child fall gentle and white
And the voice of the Christ-child tells out with delight
That mankind are the children of God.

PHILLIPS BROOKS

FOR THEM

Before you bid, for Christmas' sake,
Your guests to sit at meat,
Oh please to save a little cake
For them that have no treat.

Before you go down party-dressed
In silver gown or gold,
Oh please to send a little vest
To them that still go cold.

Before you give your girl and boy
Gay gifts to be undone,
Oh please to spare a little toy
To them that will have none.

Before you gather round the tree
To dance the day about,
Oh please to give a little glee
To them that go without.

ELEANOR FARJEON

THAT HOLY THING

They all were looking for a king
    To slay their foes and lift them high;
Thou cam'st, a little baby thing
    That made a woman cry.

O Son of Man, to right my lot
    Naught but thy presence can avail;
Yet on the road thy wheels are not,
    Nor on the sea thy sail!

39

My how or why thou wilt not heed,
But come down thine own secret stair,
That thou mayst answer all my need—
Yea, every bygone prayer.

GEORGE MACDONALD

PEACE ON EARTH

Shepherds there were who in the fields by night
Kept watch, not wisting that a chorus bright
Of angels would to them the news convey—
The dawning of the world's most potent day.

Countless the nights of darkness and of fear
The world has watched through, but the message clear
Of prophets, martyrs, saints, and poets brought
The healing word for which it blindly sought.

Visions from God—through men must come the word,
Till the whole earth to action deeply stirred
From war and dread and hatred wins release,
And hails once more as King the Prince of Peace.

HELEN WIEAND COLE

THAT HOLY STAR

O Father, may that holy Star
Grow every year more bright,
And send its glorious beam afar
To fill the world with light.

WILLIAM CULLEN BRYANT

THE MIRACLE

Into each man's life comes the miracle—
The wonder of manger and star;
But 'tis only the wise men see the light,
And the shepherds who watch afar;

And only the wise men follow its gleam
Through a desert of dusty days,

And the purple murk of appalling nights,
    And the terror of Herod-ways;

And only the shepherds hear the song
    Of "Glory to God on High;"
For their hearts are rich with humility,
    And tuned to the heavenly cry.

Yet His star is hung for all to see,
    And each has the right to bring
The gift of his soul in the palm of his hand
    To the manger that cradles the King.

For to all of the people of East and West
    Come the tidings of joy each year,
But few are the shepherds and wise men
    With the faith to see and to hear.

Into each man's life comes the miracle—
    The joy of the Christ Child's birth—
But human love alone can bring
    A second Peace to the earth.

CLAIRE S. BOYER

THE PRINCE OF PEACE

Hark! the glad sound! the Saviour comes,
    The Saviour promised long:
Let every heart prepare a throne,
    And every voice a song.

He comes, the prisoners to release
    In Satan's bondage held;
The gates of brass before Him burst,
    The iron fetters yield.

He comes, from the thick films of vice
    To clear the mental ray,
And on the eyeballs of the blind
    To pour celestial day.

41

He comes, the broken heart to bind,
   The bleeding soul to cure,
And with the treasures of His grace
   To enrich the humble poor.

Our glad hosannas, Prince of Peace,
   Thy welcome shall proclaim,
And Heaven's eternal arches ring
   With Thy beloved name.

PHILIP DODDRIDGE

THE CHRISTMAS SPIRIT

I am the Christmas Spirit.

I enter the home of poverty, causing pale-faced children to open their eyes wide in pleased wonder.

I cause the miser's clutched hand to relax, and thus paint a bright spot on his soul.

I cause the aged to renew their youth and to laugh in the glad old way.

I keep romance alive in the heart of childhood, and brighten sleep with dreams woven of magic.

I cause eager feet to climb dark stairways with filled baskets, leaving behind hearts amazed at the goodness of the world.

I cause the prodigal to pause a moment on his wild, wasteful way, and send to anxious love some little token that releases glad tears— tears which wash away the hard lines of sorrow.

I enter dark prison cells, reminding scarred manhood of what might have been, and pointing forward to good days yet to come.

I come softly into the still, white home of pain, and lips that are too weak to speak just tremble in silent, eloquent gratitude.

In a thousand ways I cause the weary world to look up into the face of God and for a little moment forget the things that are small and wretched.

I am the Christmas Spirit.

AUTHOR UNKNOWN

HIS MOTHER KEPT ALL THESE SAYINGS IN HER HEART

As o'er the cradle of her Son
The blessed Mary hung,
And chanted to the Anointed One
The psalms that David sung,

What joy her bosom must have known,
As, with a sweet surprise,
She marked the boundless love that shone
Within his infant eyes.

But deeper was her joy to hear,
Even in his ripening youth,
And treasure up, from year to year,
His words of grace and truth.

Oh, may we keep his words like her
In all their life and power,
And to the law of love refer
The acts of every hour.

WILLIAM CULLEN BRYANT

WHAT CHILD IS THIS?

What Child is this who laid to rest
On Mary's lap is sleeping,
Whom angels greet with anthems sweet
While shepherds watch are keeping?
This, this is Christ the King
Whom shepherds guard and angels sing,
Haste, haste to bring Him laud,
The Babe, the Son of Mary.

Why lies He in such mean estate
Where ox and ass are feeding?
Good Christian fear, for sinners here
The silent word is pleading.
Nails, spear shall pierce Him through.
The cross He bore for me, for you.
Hail, hail, the Lord made flesh,
The Babe, the Son of Mary.

So bring Him incense, gold and myrrh,
Come peasant, king to own Him.
The King of kings salvation brings,
Let loving hearts enthrone Him.
Raise, raise the song on high,
The virgin sings her lullaby,
Joy, joy for Christ is born.
The Babe, the Son of Mary.

W. C. DIX

Additional poems that are appropriate for Christmas appear in the topic "Jesus Christ" and elsewhere.

COURAGE

COURAGE

Courage is armor
A blind man wears;
The calloused scar
Of outlived despairs:
Courage is Fear
That has said its prayers.

KARLE WILSON BAKER

INVICTUS

Out of the night that covers me,
   Black as the pit from pole to pole,
I thank whatever gods may be
   For my unconquerable soul.

In the fell clutch of circumstance
   I have not winced nor cried aloud.
Under the bludgeonings of chance
   My head is bloody, but unbowed.

Beyond this place of wrath and tears
   Looms but the horror of the shade,
And yet the menace of the years
   Finds and shall find me unafraid.

It matters not how strait the gate,
   How charged with punishments the scroll,
I am the master of my fate:
   I am the captain of my soul.

WILLIAM ERNEST HENLEY

THE SOUL'S CAPTAIN
AN ANSWER TO "INVICTUS"

Art thou in truth?
Then what of him who bought thee with his blood?

Who plunged into devouring seas
And snatched thee from the flood?

Who bore for all our fallen race
What none but him could bear—
The God who died that man might live
And endless glory share?

Of what avail thy vaunted strength
Apart from his vast might?
Pray that his light may pierce the gloom
That thou mayest see aright.

Men are as bubbles on the wave,
As leaves upon the tree,
Thou, captain of thy soul! Forsooth,
Who gave that place to thee?

Free will is thine—free agency,
To wield for right or wrong;
But thou must answer unto him
To whom all souls belong.

Bend to the dust that "head unbowed,"
Small part of life's great whole,
And see in him and him alone,
The captain of thy soul.

ORSON F. WHITNEY

MY CAPTAIN
AN ANSWER TO "INVICTUS"

Out of the light that dazzles me,
    Bright as the sun from pole to pole,
I thank the God I know to be
    For Christ the conqueror of my soul.

Since His the sway of circumstance,
    I would not wince nor cry aloud.
Under that rule which men call chance
    My head with joy is humbly bowed.

46

Beyond this place of sin and tears
    That life with Him! And His the aid,
Despite the menace of the years,
    Keeps, and shall keep me, unafraid.

I have no fear, though strait the gate,
    He cleared from punishment the scroll.
Christ is the Master of my fate,
    Christ is the Captain of my soul.

DOROTHEA DAY

FROM MY PRAYER

We know the paths wherein our feet should press;
Across our hearts are written Thy decrees;
Yet now, O Lord, be merciful to bless
    With more than these.

Grant us the will to fashion as we feel,
Grant us the strength to labor as we know,
Grant us the purpose, ribb'd and edged with steel,
    To strike the blow.

Knowledge we ask not—knowledge Thou hast lent;
But, Lord, the will—there lies our bitter need.
Give us to build above the deep intent
    The deed, the deed.

JOHN DRINKWATER

COURAGE

I'd like to think that I can look at death and smile and say,
All I have left now is my final breath, take that away
And you must either leave me dust or dreams or in far flight
The soul that wanders where the stardust streams through endless
    night.

I'd rather think that I can look at life with this to say,
Send what you will of struggle or of strife, blue skies or gray,
I'll stand against the final charge of hate by peak and pit
And nothing in the steel clad fist of fate can make me quit.

GRANTLAND RICE

OPPORTUNITY

This I beheld, or dreamed it in a dream:
There spread a cloud of dust along a plain;
And underneath the cloud, or in it, raged
A furious battle, and men yelled, and swords
Shocked upon swords and shields. A prince's banner
Wavered, then staggered backward, hemmed by foes.
A craven hung along the battle's edge,
And thought, "Had I a sword of keener steel—
That blue blade that the king's son bears,—but this
Blunt thing!" he snapped and flung it from his hand,
And lowering crept away and left the field.
Then came the king's son, wounded, sore bestead,
And weaponless, and saw the broken sword,
Hilt-buried in the dry and trodden sand,
And ran and snatched it, and with battle-shout
Lifted afresh he hewed his enemy down,
And saved a great cause that heroic day.

EDWARD ROWLAND SILL

BUILD A LITTLE FENCE OF TRUST

Build a little fence of trust
    Around today;
Fill the space with loving works,
    And therein stay;

Look not through the sheltering bars
    Upon tomorrow,
God will help thee bear what comes
    Of joy or sorrow.

MARY FRANCES BUTTS

GOD MAKE ME A MAN

Give me the strength to stand for right
When other folks have left the fight.
Give me the courage of the man
Who knows that if he will, he can.

Teach me to see in every face
The good, the kind and not the base.
Make me sincere in word and deed
Blot out from me all shame and greed
Help me to guard my troubled soul
By constant, active self-control.
Clean up my thoughts, my work, my play
And keep me pure from day to day.
O make of me a man.

HARLAN GOLDSBURY METCALF

RIGHT MUST WIN
FROM "ON THE FIELD"

O it is hard to work for God,
    To rise and take His part
Upon this battle-field of earth,
    And not sometimes lose heart!

He hides Himself so wondrously,
    As though there were no God;
He is least seen when all the powers
    Of ill are most abroad.

Or He deserts us at the hour
    The fight is all but lost;
And seems to leave us to ourselves
    Just when we need Him most.

Ill masters good, good seems to change
    To ill with greatest ease;
And, worst of all, the good with good
    Is at cross purposes.

It is not so, but so it looks,
    And we lose courage then;
And doubts will come if God hath kept
    His promises to men.

Workman of God! oh, lose not heart,
    But learn what God is like,
And in the darkest battle-field,
    Thou shalt know where to strike.

Thrice blest is he to whom is given
    The instinct that can tell
That God is on the field when He
    Is most invisible.

Blest too is he who can divine
    Where real right doth lie,
And dares to take the side that seems
    Wrong to man's blindfold eye.

Muse on His justice, downcast soul,
    Muse, and take better heart;
Back with thine angel to the field,
    And bravely do thy part.

For right is right, since God is God,
    And right the day must win;
To doubt would be disloyalty,
    To falter would be sin.

FREDERICK WILLIAM FABER

WAITING

Serene, I fold my hands and wait,
Nor care for wind, or tide, or sea;
I rave no more 'gainst Time or Fate,
For, lo! my own shall come to me.

I stay my haste, I make delays,
For what avails this eager pace?
I stand amid the eternal ways,
And what is mine shall know my face.

Asleep, awake, by night or day,
The friends I seek are seeking me,
No wind can drive my bark astray,
Nor change the tide of destiny.

What matter if I stand alone?
I wait with joy the coming years;
My heart shall reap where it has sown,
And garner up its fruits of tears.

The waters know their own and draw
The brook that springs in yonder height:
So flows the good with equal law
Unto the soul of pure delight. . . .

The stars come nightly to the sky;
The tidal wave unto the sea;
Nor time, nor space, nor deep, nor high,
Can keep my own away from me.

JOHN BURROUGHS

Additional poems about courage appear in the topics "Adversity," "Death and Immortality," "Patriotism," and elsewhere.

DEATH AND IMMORTALITY

SHE IS NOT DEAD

She is not dead,—the child of our affection,—
    But gone unto that school
Where she no longer needs our poor protection,
    And Christ himself doth rule.

In that great cloister's stillness and seclusion,
    By guardian angels led,
Safe from temptation, safe from sin's pollution,
    She lives, whom we call dead.

Day after day we think what she is doing
    In those bright realms of air;
Year after year, her tender steps pursuing,
    Behold her grown more fair.

Thus do we walk with her, and keep unbroken
    The bond which nature gives,
Thinking that our remembrance, though unspoken,
    May reach her where she lives.

HENRY WADSWORTH LONGFELLOW

TIME

Time is
Too slow for those who wait,
Too swift for those who fear,
Too long for those who grieve,
Too short for those who rejoice;
But for those who love,
    Time is
    Eternity.

AUTHOR UNKNOWN

LITTLE BOY BLUE

The little toy dog is covered with dust,
But sturdy and staunch he stands;
And the little toy soldier is red with rust,
And his musket moulds in his hands.
Time was when the little toy dog was new,
And the soldier was passing fair,
And that was the time when our Little Boy Blue
Kissed them and put them there.

"Now, don't you go till I come," he said,
"And don't you make any noise!"
So toddling off to his trundle-bed
He dreamt of the pretty toys.
And as he was dreaming, an angel song
Awakened our Little Boy Blue,—
Oh, the years are many, the years are long,
But the little toy friends are true!

Ay, faithful to Little Boy Blue they stand,
Each in the same old place,
Awaiting the touch of a little hand,
The smile of a little face.
And they wonder, as waiting these long years through,
In the dust of that little chair,
What has become of our Little Boy Blue
Since he kissed them and put them there.

EUGENE FIELD

BREAK, BREAK, BREAK

Break, break, break
   On thy cold gray stones, O Sea!
And I would that my tongue could utter
   The thoughts that arise in me.

O well for the fisherman's boy,
   That he shouts with his sister at play!
O well for the sailor lad,
   That he sings in his boat on the bay!

53

And the stately ships go on
   To their haven under the hill;
But O for the touch of a vanish'd hand,
   And the sound of a voice that is still!

Break, break, break
   At the foot of thy crags, O Sea!
But the tender grace of a day that is dead
   Will never come back to me.

ALFRED, LORD TENNYSON

FROM WE ARE SEVEN

   A simple Child,
That lightly draws its breath,
And feels its life in every limb,
What should it know of death?

I met a little cottage Girl:
She was eight years old, she said:
Her hair was thick with many a curl
That clustered round her head.

She had a rustic, woodland air,
And she was wildly clad:
Her eyes were fair, and very fair:
—Her beauty made me glad.

"Sisters and brothers, little Maid,
How many may you be?"
"How many? Seven in all," she said,
And wondering looked at me.

"And where are they? I pray you tell."
She answered, "Seven are we;
And two of us at Conway dwell,
And two are gone to sea.

"Two of us in the church-yard lie,
My sister and my brother;
And, in the church-yard cottage, I
Dwell near them with my mother."

* * *

"How many are you, then," said I,
"If they two are in heaven?"
Quick was the little Maid's reply,
"O Master! we are seven."

"But they are dead; those two are dead!
Their spirits are in heaven!"
'Twas throwing words away; for still
The little Maid would have her will,
And said, "Nay, we are seven!"

WILLIAM WORDSWORTH

AT FIRST WHEN YOU WERE GONE

At first when you were gone I turned my face
From life and sat upon a lonely place
Apart from men, bewailed but nursed my sorrow
And, loving yesterday, I loathed tomorrow.

Then suddenly you said, "O foolish one,
 Awake, there are no dead—I *am* your own!"
And then above my sorrow and my strife
I found the Resurrection and the Life.

ROBERT NORWOOD

CHRISTUS CONSOLATOR

Beside the dead I knelt in prayer,
    And felt a presence as I prayed.
Lo! it was Jesus standing there.
    He smiled, "Be not afraid."

"Lord, thou hast conquered death, we know;
    Restore again to life," I said,
"This one who died an hour ago."
    He smiled, "She is not dead."

"Asleep, then, as thyself didst say,
    Yet thou canst lift the lids that keep
Her prisoned eyes from ours away."
    He smiled, "She doth not sleep."

55

"Nay, then, though haply she doth wake
 And look upon some fairer dawn,
Restore her to our hearts that ache."
 He smiled, "She is not gone."

"Yea, Lord we feel that she is free,
 And moves upon some higher sphere;
We are bereft; she is with thee."
 He smiled, "And I am here!"

"Dear God! how can we know that they
 Still walk unseen with us and thee,
Nor sleep, nor wander far away?"
 He smiled, "Abide in me."

ROSSITER RAYMOND

SERVANT OF GOD, WELL DONE

"Servant of God, well done;
 Rest from thy loved employ;
The battle fought, the victory won,
 Enter thy Master's joy."
The voice at midnight came;
 He started up to hear,
A mortal arrow pierced his frame:
 He fell,—but felt no fear.

Tranquil amidst alarms,
 It found him in the field,
A veteran slumbering on his arms,
 Beneath his red-cross shield:
His sword was in his hand,
 Still warm with recent fight;
Ready that moment, at command,
 Through rock and steel to smite.

At midnight came the cry,
 "To meet thy God prepare!"
He woke,—and caught his Captain's eye;
 Then, strong in faith and prayer,
His spirit, with a bound,
 Burst its encumbering clay;

His tent, at sunrise, on the ground,
  A darkened ruin lay.

The pains of death are past,
  Labor and sorrow cease;
And life's long warfare closed at last,
  His soul is found in peace.
Soldier of Christ! well done;
  Praise be thy new employ;
And while eternal ages run,
  Rest in thy Saviour's joy.

JAMES MONTGOMERY

WHENCE THIS PLEASING HOPE

Whence this pleasing hope, this fond desire,
  This longing for immortality?
'Tis the divinity that stirs within us;
'Tis heaven itself that points out an hereafter,
  And intimates eternity to man.

JOSEPH ADDISON

BEYOND THIS VALE OF TEARS

Beyond this vale of tears,
  There is a life above,
Unmeasured by the flight of years;
  And all that life is love.

JAMES MONTGOMERY

HEAVEN

Think of
Stepping on shore, and finding it Heaven!
Of taking hold of a hand, and finding it God's hand.
Of breathing a new air, and finding it celestial air.
Of feeling invigorated, and finding it immortality.
Of passing from storm to tempest to an unbroken calm.
Of waking up, and finding it Home.

AUTHOR UNKNOWN

UPHILL

Does the road wind uphill all the way?
    Yes, to the very end.
Will the day's journey take the whole long day?
    From morn to night, my friend.

But is there for the night a resting-place?
    A roof for when the slow dark hours begin.
May not the darkness hide it from my face?
    You cannot miss that inn.

Shall I meet other wayfarers at night?
    Those who have gone before.
Then must I knock, or call when just in sight?
    They will not keep you standing at that door.

Shall I find comfort, travel-sore and weak?
    Of labor you shall find the sum.
Will there be beds for me and all who seek?
    Yea, beds for all who come.

CHRISTINA ROSSETTI

DEATH, BE NOT PROUD

Death, be not proud, though some have called thee
Mighty and dreadful, for thou art not so;
For those whom thou think'st thou dost overthrow
Die not, poor Death; nor yet canst thou kill me.
From rest and sleep, which but thy pictures be,
Much pleasure; then from thee much more must flow;
And soonest our best men with thee do go—
Rest of their bones and souls' delivery!
Thou art slave to fate, chance, kings, and desperate men,
And dost with poison, war, and sickness dwell;
And poppy or charms can make us sleep as well
And better than thy stroke. Why swell'st thou then?
One short sleep past, we wake eternally,
And Death shall be no more: Death, thou shalt die!

JOHN DONNE

From SNOW-BOUND

And yet, dear heart! remembering thee,
　Am I not richer than of old?
Safe in thy immortality,
　What change can reach the wealth I hold?
What chance can mar the pearl and gold
　Thy love hath left in trust for me?

And while in life's long afternoon,
　Where cool and long the shadows grow,
I walk to meet the night that soon
　Shall shape and shadow overflow,
I cannot feel that thou art far,
　Since near at need the angels are;

And when the sunset gates unbar,
　Shall I not see thee waiting stand,
And, white against the evening star,
　The welcome of thy beckoning hand?

JOHN GREENLEAF WHITTIER

DEAREST SISTER

Dearest sister, thou hast left us,
　And thy loss we deeply feel,
Yet 'tis God that has bereft us,
　He can all our sorrows heal.

Yet again we hope to see thee,
　When death's gloomy night has fled,
Then on earth with joy to greet thee,
　Where no bitter tears are shed.

ANNE SAWYER

From THE CHAMBERED NAUTILUS

Build thee more stately mansions, O my soul,
As the swift seasons roll!
Leave thy low-vaulted past!
Let each new temple, nobler than the last,

Shut thee from heaven with a dome more vast,
Till thou at length art free,
Leaving thine outgrown shell by life's unresting sea!

OLIVER WENDELL HOLMES

WHAT OF DEATH?

Ay! it will come,—the bitter hour!—but bringing
A better love beyond, more subtle-sweet;
A higher road to tread, with happier singing,
And no cross-ways to part familiar feet!

SIR EDWIN ARNOLD

PROSPICE

Fear death?—to feel the fog in my throat,
The mist in my face,
When the snows begin, and the blasts denote
I am nearing the place,
The power of the night, the press of the storm,
The post of the foe;
Where he stands, the Arch Fear in a visible form,
Yet the strong man must go.
For the journey is done and the summit attained,
And the barriers fall,
Though a battle's to fight ere the [great prize] be gained,
The reward of it all.
I was ever a fighter, so—one fight more,
The best and the last!
I would hate that death bandaged my eyes, and forbore,
And bade me creep past.
No! let me taste the whole of it, fare like my peers,
The heroes of old,
Bear the brunt, in a minute pay glad life's arrears
Of pain, darkness, and cold.
For sudden the worst turns the best to the brave,
The black minute's at end,
And the elements' rage, the fiend-voices that rave,
Shall dwindle, shall blend,
Shall change, shall become first a peace out of pain,
Then a light, then thy breast,

O thou soul of my soul! I shall clasp thee again,
   And with God be the rest!

ROBERT BROWNING

FAREWELL, DEAR SISTER

Farewell, dear sister, we shall meet no more
Till we arrive on Canaan's happy shore;
There we shall meet at our Redeemer's seat,
And cast our crowns of victory at His feet.

J. BAILEY

CONSOLATION

He is not dead, this friend; not dead,
But, in the path we mortals tread,
Gone some few, trifling steps ahead,
   And nearer to the end;
So that you, too, once past the bend,
Shall meet again, as face to face, this friend
   You fancy dead.

ROBERT LOUIS STEVENSON

THE CHARIOT

Because I could not stop for Death,
He kindly stopped for me;
The carriage held but just ourselves
And Immortality.

We slowly drove, he knew no haste,
And I had put away
My labor, and my leisure too,
For his civility.

We passed the school where children played,
Their lessons scarcely done;
We passed the fields of gazing grain,
We passed the setting sun.

61

We paused before a house that seemed
A swelling on the ground;
The roof was scarcely visible,
The cornice but a mound.

Since then 'tis centuries; but each
Feels shorter than the day
I first surmised the horses' heads
Were toward eternity.

EMILY DICKINSON

BE YE ALSO READY
FROM "THANATOPSIS"

So live, that when thy summons comes to join
The innumerable caravan, which moves
To that mysterious realm, where each shall take
His chamber in the silent halls of death,
Thou go not, like the quarry-slave at night,
Scourged to his dungeon, but, sustained and soothed
By an unfaltering trust, approach thy grave,
Like one who wraps the drapery of his couch
About him, and lies down to pleasant dreams.

WILLIAM CULLEN BRYANT

NATURE

As a fond mother, when the day is o'er,
    Leads by the hand her little child to bed,
    Half willing, half reluctant to be led,
    And leave his broken playthings on the floor,
Still gazing at them through the open door,
    Nor wholly reassured and comforted
    By promises of others in their stead,
    Which, though more splendid, may not please him more;
So Nature deals with us, and takes away
    Our playthings one by one, and by the hand
    Leads us to rest so gently, that we go
Scarce knowing if we wish to go or stay,
    Being too full of sleep to understand
    How far the unknown transcends the what we know.

HENRY WADSWORTH LONGFELLOW

WHEN SINKS THE SOUL

When sinks the soul, subdued by toil to slumber,
    Its closing eyes look up to thee in prayer,
Sweet the repose beneath thy [arms] o'ershading
    But sweeter still to wake and find thee there.

So shall it be at last in that bright morning
    When the soul waketh, and life's shadows flee,
O in that hour, fairer than daylight's dawning,
    Shall rise the glorious thought, I am with thee—
Still, still with thee.

HARRIET BEECHER STOWE

WELCOME

Here in this world
He bids us come,
There in the next
He shall bid us welcome.

JOHN DONNE

WHEN EARTH'S LAST PICTURE IS PAINTED

When Earth's last picture is painted, and the tubes are twisted and
    dried,
When the oldest colours have faded, and the youngest critic has died,
We shall rest, and, faith, we shall need it—lie down for an aeon or
    two,
Till the Master of All Good Workmen shall put us to work anew.

And those that were good shall be happy: they shall sit in a golden
    chair;
They shall splash at a ten-league canvas with brushes of comets' hair;
They shall find real saints to draw from—Magdalene, Peter, and Paul;
They shall work for an age at a sitting, and never be tired at all!

And only the Master shall praise us, and only the Master shall blame;
And no one shall work for money, and no one shall work for fame,
But each for the joy of the working, and each, in his separate star,
Shall draw the Thing as he sees It for the God of Things as They Are!

RUDYARD KIPLING

63

BENJAMIN FRANKLIN'S EPITAPH

Like the cover of an old book,
Its contents torn out
And stripped of its lettering and gilding,
Lies here food for worms.
But the work shall not be lost,
For it will—as he believes—appear once more
In a new and more elegant edition,
Revised and corrected by the Author.

BENJAMIN FRANKLIN

CROSSING THE BAR

Sunset and evening star,
    And one clear call for me,
And may there be no moaning of the bar,
    When I put out to sea.

But such a tide as moving seems asleep,
    Too full for sound and foam,
When that which drew from out the boundless deep
    Turns again home.

Twilight and evening bell,
    And after that the dark!
And may there be no sadness of farewell,
    When I embark;

For tho' from out our bourne of Time and Place
    The flood may bear me far,
I hope to see my Pilot face to face
    When I have crossed the bar.

ALFRED, LORD TENNYSON

Additional poems about death and immortality appear in the topics "Faith," "Jesus Christ," "Memorial Day," and elsewhere.

DIVINE NATURE

FROM ODE ON INTIMATIONS OF IMMORTALITY

Our birth is but a sleep and a forgetting:
The Soul that rises with us, our life's Star,
Hath had elsewhere its setting,
And cometh from afar:
Not in entire forgetfulness,
And not in utter nakedness,
But trailing clouds of glory do we come
From God, who is our home.

WILLIAM WORDSWORTH

MY MIND TO ME A KINGDOM IS

My mind to me a kingdom is,
Such present joys therein I find,
That it excels all other bliss
That earth affords or grows by kind.

SIR EDWARD DYER

THE IMAGE OF GOD

O Lord! who seest from yon starry height,
Centred in one the future and the past,
Fashioned in thine own image, see how fast
The world obscures in me what once was bright!
Eternal sun! the warmth which thou hast given,
To cheer life's flowery April, fast decays;
Yet in the hoary winter of my days,
Forever green shall be my trust in heaven.
Celestial King! oh, let thy presence pass
Before my spirit, and an image fair
Shall meet that look of mercy from on high,
As the reflected image in a glass
Doth meet the look of him who seeks it there,
And owes its being to the gazer's eye.

FRANCESCO DE ALDANA,
TRANS. HENRY WADSWORTH LONGFELLOW

I WOULD BE TRUE

I would be true, for there are those who trust me;
I would be pure, for there are those who care;
I would be strong, for there is much to suffer;
I would be brave, for there is much to dare.

I would be friend of all—the foe, the friendless;
I would be giving, and forget the gift;
I would be humble, for I know my weakness;
I would look up—and laugh, and love, and lift.

HOWARD ARNOLD WALTER

A PRAYER FOR EVERY DAY

Make me too brave to lie or be unkind.
Make me too understanding, too, to mind
The little hurts companions give, and friends,
The careless hurts that no one quite intends.
Make me too thoughtful to hurt others so.
Help me to know
The inmost hearts of those for whom I care,
Their secret wishes, all the loads they bear,
That I may add my courage to their own.
May I make lonely folks feel less alone,
And happy ones a little happier yet.
May I forget
What ought to be forgotten; and recall
Unfailing, all
That ought to be recalled, each kindly thing,
Forgetting what might sting.
To all upon my way,
Day after day,
Let me be joy, be hope! Let my life sing!

MARY CAROLYN DAVIES

THE BIRD LET LOOSE

The bird let loose in eastern skies,
    When hastening fondly home,
Ne'er stoops to earth her wing, nor flies
    Where idle warblers roam;

But high she shoots through air and light,
   Above all low delay,
Where nothing earthly bounds her flight,
   Nor shadow dims her way.

So grant me, God, from every care
   And stain of passion free,
Aloft, through Virtue's purer air,
   To hold my course to thee!
No sin to cloud, no lure to stay
   My soul, as home she springs;—
Thy sunshine on her joyful way,
   Thy freedom in her wings!

THOMAS MOORE

SHE WALKS IN BEAUTY

She walks in beauty, like the night
   Of cloudless climes and starry skies;
And all that's best of dark and bright
   Meet in her aspect and her eyes:
Thus mellow'd to that tender light
   Which heaven to gaudy day denies.

One shade the more, one ray the less,
   Had half impair'd the nameless grace
Which waves in every raven tress,
   Or softly lightens o'er her face;
Where thoughts serenely sweet express
   How pure, how dear their dwelling-place.

And on that cheek, and o'er that brow,
   So soft, so calm, yet eloquent,
The smiles that win, the tints that glow,
   But tell of days in goodness spent,
A mind at peace with all below,
   A heart whose love is innocent!

LORD BYRON

*Additional poems about divine nature appear in the topics "Character,"
"Integrity," and elsewhere.*

EASTER

TOMB, THOU SHALT NOT HOLD HIM LONGER

Tomb, thou shalt not hold him longer;
Death is strong, but Life is stronger;
Stronger than the dark, the light;
Stronger than the wrong, the right;
Faith and Hope triumphant say
Christ will rise on Easter Day.

PHILLIPS BROOKS

FROM AN EASTER CANTICLE

In every trembling bud and bloom
    That cleaves the earth, a flowery sword,
I see Thee come from out the tomb,
    Thou risen Lord.

* * *

Thou art not dead! Thou art the whole
    Of life that quickens in the sod;
Green April is Thy very soul,
    Thou great Lord God.

CHARLES HANSON TOWNE

RESURRECTION

In this brown seed, so dry and hard,
I see a flower in my door yard.
You, chrysalis in winding sheet,
Are butterfly all dainty sweet.
All life is warmed by spring's sweet breath,
And Christ our Lord has conquered death.

AGNES W. STORER

ON A GLOOMY EASTER

I hear the robins singing in the rain.
   The longed-for Spring is hushed so drearily
   That hungry lips cry often wearily,
"Oh, if the blessed sun would shine again!"

I hear the robins singing in the rain.
   The misty world lies waiting for the dawn;
   The wind sobs at my window and is gone,
And in the silence come old throbs of pain.

But still the robins sing on in the rain,
   Not waiting for the morning sun to break,
   Nor listening for the violets to wake,
Nor fearing lest the snow may fall again.

My heart sings with the robins in the rain,
   For I remember it is Easter morn,
   And life and love and peace are all new born,
And joy has triumphed over loss and pain.

Sing on, brave robins, sing on in the rain!
   You know behind the clouds the sun must shine,
   You know that death means only life divine
And all our losses turn to heavenly gain.

I lie and listen to you in the rain.
   Better than Easter bells that do not cease,
   Your message from the heart of God's great peace,
And to his arms I turn and sleep again.

ALICE FREEMAN PALMER

IF EASTER BE NOT TRUE

   If Easter be not true,
Then all the lilies low must lie;
The Flanders poppies fade and die;
The spring must lose her fairest bloom
For Christ were still within the tomb—
   If Easter be not true.

If Easter be not true,
Then faith must mount on broken wing;
Then hope no more immortal spring;
Then hope must lose her mighty urge;
Life prove a phantom, death a dirge—
    If Easter be not true.

If Easter be not true,
'Twere foolishness the cross to bear;
He died in vain who suffered there;
What matter though we laugh or cry,
Be good or evil, live or die,
    If Easter be not true?

If Easter be not true—
But it is true, and Christ is risen!
And mortal spirit from its prison
Of sin and death with him may rise!
Worthwhile the struggle, sure the prize,
    Since Easter, aye, is true!

HENRY H. BARSTOW

EASTER

Sing, soul of mine, this day of days.
    The Lord is risen.
Toward the sunrising set thy face.
    The Lord is risen.
Behold he giveth strength and grace;
For darkness, light; for mourning, praise;
For sin, his holiness; for conflict, peace.

Arise, O soul, this Easter Day!
Forget the tomb of yesterday,
For thou from bondage art set free;
Thou sharest in his victory
And life eternal is for thee,
Because the Lord is risen.

AUTHOR UNKNOWN

A SONG AT EASTER

If this bright lily
  Can live once more,
And its white promise
  Be as before,
Why can not the great stone
  Be moved from His door?

If the green grass
  Ascend and shake
Year after year,
  And blossoms break
Again and again
  For April's sake,

Why can not He,
  From the dark and mould,
Show us again
  His manifold
And gleaming glory,
  A stream of gold?

Faint heart, be sure
  These things must be.
See the new bud
  On the old tree! . . .
If flowers can wake,
  Oh, why not He?

CHARLES HANSON TOWNE

THE STRIFE IS O'ER

The strife is o'er, the battle done;
The victory of life is won;
The song of triumph has begun.
  Alleluia!

The powers of death have done their worst,
But Christ their legions hath dispersed;
Let shouts of holy joy outburst.
  Alleluia!

The three sad days are quickly sped;
He rises glorious from the dead;
All glory to our risen Head!
   Alleluia!

He closed the yawning gates of hell;
The bars from heaven's high portals fell;
Let hymns of praise his triumph tell!
   Alleluia!

Lord! by the stripes which wounded thee,
From death's dread sting thy servants free,
That we may live and sing to thee!
   Alleluia!

AUTHOR UNKNOWN, TRANS. FRANCIS POTTS

AN EASTER WISH

May the glad dawn
   Of Easter morn
   Bring joy to thee.

May the calm eve
   Of Easter leave
   A peace divine with thee.

May Easter night
   On thine heart write,
   O Christ, I live for thee!

AUTHOR UNKNOWN

Additional poems that are appropriate for Easter appear in the topics "Death and Immortality," "Jesus Christ," and elsewhere.

EXAMPLE

YOU NEVER TALKED RELIGION

You never talked religion, friend;
   You never spoke of any creed;
You never queried of life's end,
   There seemed no need.
You never chided me for aught,
   Nor proudly claimed a higher place
In principles and yet you taught
   Of heavenly grace.
You passed along life's workaday
   With God set first—your neighbor next
And all things selfish out away—
   You lived your text.

AUTHOR UNKNOWN

ACCEPT MY FULL HEART'S THANKS

Your words came just when needed.
Like a breeze,
Blowing and bringing from the wide salt sea
Some cooling spray, to meadow scorched with heat
And choked with dust and clouds of sifted sand . . .
So words of thine came over miles to me,
Fresh from the mighty sea, a true friend's heart,
And brought me hope, and strength, and swept away
The dusty webs that human spiders spun
Across my path. Friend—and the word means much—
So few there are who reach like thee, a hand
Up over all the barking curs of spite
And give the clasp, when most its need is felt,
Friend, newly found, accept my full heart's thanks.

ELLA WHEELER WILCOX

BE SUCH A MAN

Be such a man, and live such a life,
That if every man were such as you,
And every life a life like yours,
This earth would be God's Paradise.

PHILLIPS BROOKS

THE GLORY OF LOVE IS BRIGHTER

The glory of love is brighter
    When the glory of self is dim;
And they have most compelled me
    Who most have pointed to Him;
They have held me, stirred me, swayed me—
    I have hung on their every word
Till I fain would rise and follow
    Not them, not them, but their Lord.

RUBY T. WEYBURN

THE CALF-PATH

One day through the primeval wood
A calf walked home as good calves should;
But made a trail all bent askew,
A crooked path as all calves do.

The trail was taken up next day
By a lone dog that passed that way;
And then a wise bellwether sheep
Pursued the trail o'er vale and steep,
And drew the flock behind him, too,
As good bellwethers always do.
And from that day, o'er hill and glade,
Through those old woods a path was made.

And many men wound in and out,
And dodged and turned and bent about,
And uttered words of righteous wrath
Because 'twas such a crooked path; . . .

The forest path became a lane
That bent and turned and turned again:
This crooked lane became a road,
Where many a poor horse with his load
Toiled on beneath the burning sun,
And traveled some three miles in one. . . .

The years passed on in swiftness fleet,
The road became a village street;
And this, before men were aware,
A city's crowded thoroughfare. . . .

Each day a hundred thousand rout
Followed this zigzag calf about
And o'er his crooked journey went
The traffic of a continent.
A hundred thousand men were led
By one calf near three centuries dead.
They followed still his crooked way,
And lost one hundred years a day;
For thus such reverence is lent
To well-established precedent.

For men are prone to go it blind
Along the calf-path of the mind,
And work away from sun to sun
To do what other men have done.
They follow in the beaten track,
And out and in, and forth and back,
And still their devious course pursue,
To keep the path that others do.
They keep the path a sacred groove,
Along which all their lives they move;
But how the wise old wood-gods laugh,
Who saw the first primeval calf.

SAM WALTER FOSS

YOUR OWN VERSION

You are writing a Gospel,
A chapter each day,
By deeds that you do,
By words that you say.

Men read what you write,
    Whether faithless or true;
Say, what is the Gospel
    According to you?

PAUL GILBERT

SERMON WITHOUT WORDS

Saint Francis came to preach. With smiles he met
The friendless, fed the poor, freed a trapped bird,
Led home a child. Although he spoke no word,
His text, God's love, the town did not forget.

ELIZABETH PATTON MOSS

BRIGHTLY BEAMS OUR FATHER'S MERCY

Brightly beams our Father's mercy
From his lighthouse evermore,
But to us he gives the keeping
Of the lights along the shore.

Dark the night of sin has settled;
Loud the angry billows roar.
Eager eyes are watching, longing,
For the lights along the shore.

Trim your feeble lamp, my brother;
Some poor sailor, tempest-tossed,
Trying now to make the harbor,
In the darkness may be lost.

Let the lower lights be burning;
Send a gleam across the wave.
Some poor fainting, struggling seaman
You may rescue, you may save.

PHILIP PAUL BLISS

IF . . .

If a child lives with criticism, he learns to condemn.
If a child lives with hostility, he learns to fight.

If a child lives with fears, he learns to be apprehensive.
If a child lives with pity, he learns to feel sorry for himself.
If a child lives with jealousy, he learns to feel guilty.
If a child lives with encouragement, he learns to be confident.
If a child lives with tolerance, he learns to be patient.
If a child lives with praise, he learns to be appreciative.
If a child lives with acceptance, he learns to love.
If a child lives with approval, he learns to like himself.
If a child lives with recognition, he learns to have a goal.
If a child lives with fairness, he learns what justice is.
If a child lives with honesty, he learns what truth is.
If a child lives with security, he learns to have faith in himself
    and in those about him.
If a child lives with friendliness, he learns that the world is
    a good place in which to live.

THE WATCHMAN-EXAMINER

PARENTS MAY TELL

Parents may tell
But never teach
Unless they practice
What they preach.

AUTHOR UNKNOWN

*Additional poems about example appear in the topics "Character,"
"Friendship," "Teaching," and elsewhere.*

FAITH

I NEVER SAW A MOOR

I never saw a moor,
I never saw the sea;
Yet know I how the heather looks,
And what a wave must be.

I never spoke with God,
Nor visited in heaven;
Yet certain am I of the spot
As if the chart were given.

EMILY DICKINSON

O WORLD

O world, thou choosest not the better part!
It is not wisdom to be only wise,
And on the inward vision close the eyes;
But it is wisdom to believe the heart.
Columbus found a world and had no chart,
Save one that faith deciphered in the skies.
To trust the soul's invincible surmise
Was all his science and his only art.
Our knowledge is a torch of smoky pine
That lights the pathway but one step ahead
Across a void of mystery and dread.
Bid, then, the tender light of faith to shine
By which alone the mortal heart is led
Unto the thinking of the thought divine.

GEORGE SANTAYANA

FAITH

I believe in the world and its bigness and splendor:
That most of the hearts beating round us are tender;
That days are but footsteps and years are but miles
That lead us to beauty and singing and smiles:

That roses that blossom and toilers that plod
Are filled with the glorious spirit of God.

I believe in the purpose of everything living:
That taking is but the forerunner of giving;
That strangers are friends that we some day may meet;
And not all the bitter can equal the sweet;
That creeds are but colors, and no man has said
That God loves the yellow rose more than the red.

I believe in the path that to-day I am treading,
That I shall come safe through the dangers I'm dreading;
That even the scoffer shall turn from his ways
And some day be won back to trust and to praise;
That the lead on the tree and the thing we call Man
Are sharing alike in His infinite plan.

I believe that all things that are living and breathing
Some richness of beauty to earth are bequeathing;
That all that goes out of this world leaves behind
Some duty accomplished for mortals to find;
That the humblest of creatures our praise is deserving,
For it, with the wisest, the Master is serving.

EDGAR A. GUEST

IF YOU TRUST

If you trust, you will not worry;
If you worry, you do not trust.

AUTHOR UNKNOWN

PASSIVE FAITH

Passive Faith but praises in the light,
   When sun doth shine.
Active Faith will praise in darkest night—
   Which faith is thine?

AUTHOR UNKNOWN

I RAISED MY EYES

I raised my eyes to yonder heights
And longed for lifting wings
To bear me to their sunlit crests,
As on my spirit sings.
And though my feet must keep the paths
That wind along the valley's floor,
Yet after every upward glance
I'm stronger than before.

AUTHOR UNKNOWN

STRONG SON OF GOD
FROM *IN MEMORIAM*

Strong Son of God, immortal Love,
    Whom we, that have not seen thy face,
    By faith, and faith alone, embrace,
Believing where we cannot prove;

* * *

We have but faith: we cannot know,
    For knowledge is of things we see;
    And yet we trust it comes from thee,
A beam in darkness: let it grow.

ALFRED, LORD TENNYSON

EYE'S NOT SEEN THE UNTOLD TREASURES

Eye's not seen the untold treasures,
    Which the Father hath in store,
Teeming with surpassing pleasures,
    Even life for evermore!

AUTHOR UNKNOWN

DO YOUR DUTY

Do your duty, that is best,
Leave unto the Lord the rest.

AUTHOR UNKNOWN

RELIGIO LAICI

Dim as the borrow'd beams of moon and stars
To lonely, weary, wand'ring travelers,
Is Reason to the soul; and, as on high
Those rolling fires discover but the sky,
Not light us here, so reason's glimmering ray
Was lent, not to assure our doubtful way,
But guide us upward to a better day.
And as those nightly tapers disappear,
When day's bright lord ascends our hemisphere;
So pale grows Reason at Religion's sight;
So dies, and so dissolves in supernatural light.

JOHN DRYDEN

TRUST IN GOD AND DO THE RIGHT

Courage, brother, do not stumble,
Though thy path is dark as night;
There's a star to guide the humble—
Trust in God and do the right.

Let the road be long and dreary,
And its ending out of sight,
Foot it bravely—strong or weary,
Trust in God and do the right.

Perish "policy" and cunning,
Perish all that fears the light;
Whether losing, whether winning,
Trust in God and do the right.

Some will hate thee, some will love thee,
Some will flatter, some will slight,
Turn from man, and look above thee,
Trust in God and do the right.

Simple rule and safest guiding,
Inward peace and inward light,
Star upon our path abiding,
Trust in God and do the right.

AUTHOR UNKNOWN

81

BALLAD OF THE TEMPEST

We were crowded in the cabin,
Not a soul would dare to sleep,—
It was midnight on the waters,
And a storm was on the deep.

'Tis a fearful thing in winter
To be shattered by the blast,
And to hear the rattling trumpet
Thunder, "Cut away the mast!"

So we shuddered there in silence,—
For the stoutest held his breath,
While the hungry sea was roaring
And the breakers talked with death.

As thus we sat in darkness,
Each one busy with his prayers,
"We are lost!" the captain shouted,
As he staggered down the stairs.

But his little daughter whispered,
As she took his icy hand,
"Isn't God upon the ocean,
Just the same as on the land?"

Then we kissed the little maiden,
And we spake in better cheer,
And we anchored safe in harbor
When the morn was shining clear.

JAMES THOMAS FIELDS

WHICHEVER WAY THE WIND DOTH BLOW

Whichever way the wind doth blow
Some heart is glad to have it so;
Then blow it east or blow it west,
The wind that blows, that wind is best.

My little craft sails not alone;
A thousand fleets from every zone
Are out upon a thousand seas;
And what for me were favouring breeze

Might dash another, with the shock
Of doom, upon some hidden rock.
And so I do not dare to pray
For winds to waft me on my way,
But leave it to a Higher Will
To stay or speed me; trusting still
That all is well, and sure that He
Who launched my bark will sail with me
Through storm and calm, and will not fail
Whatever breezes may prevail
To land me, every peril past,
Within His sheltering Heaven at last.

Then whatsoever wind doth blow,
My heart is glad to have it so;
And blow it east or blow it west,
The wind that blows, that wind is best.

CAROLINE ATHERTON MASON

BE STILL, MY SOUL

Be still, my soul: The Lord is on thy side;
With patience bear thy cross of grief or pain.
Leave to thy God to order and provide;
In ev'ry change he faithful will remain.
Be still, my soul: Thy best, thy heav'nly Friend
Thru thorny ways leads to a joyful end.

Be still, my soul: Thy God doth undertake
To guide the future as he has the past.
Thy hope, thy confidence let nothing shake;
All now mysterious shall be bright at last.
Be still, my soul: The waves and winds still know
His voice who ruled them while he dwelt below.

Be still, my soul: The hour is hast'ning on
When we shall be forever with the Lord,
When disappointment, grief, and fear are gone,
Sorrow forgot, love's purest joys restored.
Be still, my soul: When change and tears are past,
All safe and blessed we shall meet at last.

KATHARINA VON SCHLEGEL, TRANS. JANE BORTHWICK

IF FAITH PRODUCE NOT WORKS

If faith produce not works, I see
That faith is not a living tree.
Thus faith and works together grow,
No separate life they e'er may know.
They're soul and body, hand and heart,
What God hath joined, let no man part.

AUTHOR UNKNOWN

SO KEEP YOUR FAITH IN GOD ABOVE

So keep your faith in God above,
And faith in the righteous truth;
It shall bring you back to the absent love,
And the joys of a vanished youth.

You shall smile once more when your tears are dried,
Meet trouble and swiftly rout it,
For faith is the strength of the soul inside,
And lost is the man without it.

AUTHOR UNKNOWN

FAITH

I will not doubt, though all my ships at sea
    Come drifting home with broken masts and sails;
    I shall believe the Hand which never fails,
From seeming evil worketh good to me;
    And, though I weep because those sails are battered,
    Still will I cry, while my best hopes lie shattered,
        "I trust in Thee."

I will not doubt, though all my prayers return
    Unanswered from the still, white realm above;
    I shall believe it is an all-wise Love
Which has refused those things for which I yearn;
    And though, at times, I cannot keep from grieving,
    Yet the pure ardor of my fixed believing
        Undimmed shall burn.

I will not doubt, though sorrows fall like rain,
  And troubles swarm like bees about a hive;
  I shall believe the heights for which I strive,
Are only reached by anguish and by pain;
  And, though I groan and tremble with my crosses,
  I yet shall see, through my severest losses,
    The greater gain.

I will not doubt; well anchored in the faith,
  Like some stanch ship, my soul braves every gale,
  So strong its courage that it will not fail
To breast the mighty, unknown sea of death.
  Oh, may I cry when body parts with spirit,
  "I do not doubt," so listening worlds may hear it
    With my last breath.

ELLA WHEELER WILCOX

Additional poems about faith appear in the topics "Adversity," "God," "Hope," and elsewhere.

FATHERHOOD

THAT BOY

He wants to be like his dad! you men,
Did you ever think, as you pause,
That the boy who watches your every move
Is building a set of laws?
He's molding a life you're the model for,
And whether it's good or bad
Depends upon the kind of example set
To the boy who'd be like his dad.

Would you have him go everywhere you go?
Have him do just the things you do?
And see everything that your eyes behold,
And woo all the gods you woo?
When you see the worship that shines in the eyes
Of your lovable little lad,
Could you rest content if he gets his wish
And grows to be like his dad?

It's a job that none but yourself can fill;
It's a charge you must answer for;
It's a duty to show him the road to tread
Ere he reaches his manhood's door.
It's a debt you owe for the greatest joy
On this earth to be had:
The pleasure of having a boy to raise
Who wants to be like his dad!

AUTHOR UNKNOWN

HIS EXAMPLE

There are little eyes upon you, and they're watching night and day;
There are little ears that quickly take in every word you say;
There are little hands all eager to do everything you do,
And a little boy that's dreaming of the day he'll be like you.

You're the little fellow's idol, you're the wisest of the wise;
In his little mind about you no suspicions ever rise;
He believes in you devoutly, holds that all you say and do
He will say and do in your way when he's grown up just like you.

Oh, it sometimes makes me shudder when I hear my boy repeat
Some careless phrase I've uttered in the language of the street;
And it sets my heart to grieving when some little fault I see
And I know beyond all doubting that he picked it up from me.

There's a wide-eyed little fellow who believes you're always right,
And his ears are always open and he watches day and night;
You are setting an example every day in all you do
For the little boy who's waiting to grow up to be like you.

EDGAR A. GUEST

TO MY UNBORN SON

"My son!" What simple, beautiful words!
    "My boy!" What a wonderful phrase!
We're counting the months till you come to us—
    The months, and the weeks, and the days!

"The new little stranger," some babes are called,
    But that's not what you're going to be;
With double my virtues and half of my faults,
    You can't be a stranger to me!

Your mother is straight as a sapling plant,
    The cleanest and best of her clan—
You're bone of her bone, and flesh of her flesh,
    And, by heaven, we'll make you a man!

Soon I shall take you in two strong arms—
    You that shall howl for joy—
With a simple, passionate, wonderful pride
    Because you are just—my boy!

And you shall lie in your mother's arms,
    And croon at your mother's breast,
And I shall thank God I am there to shield
    The two that I love the best.

A wonderful thing is a breaking wave,
    And sweet is the scent of spring,
But the silent voice of an unborn babe
    Is God's most beautiful thing.

We're listening now to that silent voice
    And waiting, your mother and I—
Waiting to welcome that fruit of our love
    When you come to us by and by.

We're hungry to show you a wonderful world
    With wonderful things to be done,
We're aching to give you the best of us both
    And we're lonely for you—my son!

CYRIL MORTON THORNE

TWO PRAYERS

Last night my little boy confessed to me
Some childish wrong;
And kneeling at my knee,
He prayed with tears—
"Dear God, make me a man
Like Daddy—wise and strong;
I know you can."

Then while he slept
I knelt beside his bed,
Confessed my sins,
And prayed with low-bowed head—
"O God, make me a child
Like my child here—
Pure, guileless,
Trusting Thee with faith sincere."

ANDREW GILLIES

WHAT MAKES A DAD?

God took the strength of a mountain,
    The majesty of a tree,
The warmth of a summer sun,
    The calm of a quiet sea,

88

The generous soul of nature,
   The comforting arm of night,
The wisdom of the ages,
   The power of the eagles' flight,
The joy of a morning in spring,
   The faith of a mustard seed,
The patience of eternity,
   The depth of a family need.
Then God combined these qualities;
   There was nothing more to add.
He knew His masterpiece was complete,
   And so He called it Dad.

AUTHOR UNKNOWN

FINE

Isn't it fine when the day is done,
And the petty battles are lost or won,
When the gold is made and the ink is dried,
To quit the struggle and turn aside
To spend an hour with your boy in play,
And let him race all of your cares away?

Isn't it fine when the day's gone well,
When you have glorious tales to tell,
And your heart is light and your head is high,
For nothing has happened to make you sigh,
To hurry homewards to share the joy
That your work has won with a little boy?

Isn't it fine, whether good or bad
Has come to the hopes and the plans you had,
And the day is over, to find him there,
Thinking you splendid and just and fair,
Ready to chase all your griefs away,
And soothe your soul with an hour of play?

Oh, whether the day's been long or brief,
Whether it's brought to me joy or grief,
Whether I've failed, or whether I've won,
It shall matter not when the work is done;

I shall count it fine if I end each day
With a little boy in an hour of play.

EDGAR A. GUEST

TO BE HONEST

To be honest, to be kind;
To earn a little and to spend a little less;
To make upon the whole a family happier for his presence;
To renounce when that shall be necessary and not to be embittered;
To keep a few friends, but those without capitulation,—
Above all, on the same grim conditions, to keep friends with
    himself—
Here is a task for all that a man has of fortitude and delicacy.

ROBERT LOUIS STEVENSON

I FOLLOW A FAMOUS FATHER

I follow a famous father,
His honor is mine to wear;
He gave me a name that was free from shame,
A name he was proud to bear.

I follow a famous father,
And him I must keep in mind;
Though his form is gone, I must carry on
The name that he left behind.

EDGAR A. GUEST

ONLY A DAD

Only a dad with a tired face,
Coming home from the daily race,
Bringing little of gold or fame
To show how well he has played the game,
But glad in his heart that his own rejoice
To see him come home and to hear his voice.

Only a dad with a brood of four,
One of ten million or more
Plodding along in the daily strife,

90

Bearing the whips and the scorns of life,
With never a whimper of pain or hate,
For the sake of those who at home await.

Only a dad, neither rich nor proud,
Merely one of the surging crowd,
Toiling, striving from day to day,
Facing whatever may come his way,
Silent whenever the harsh condemn,
And bearing it all for the love of them.

Only a dad, but he gives his all
To smooth the way for his children small,
Doing with courage stern and grim
The deeds that his father did for him.
This is the line that for him I pen:
Only a dad, but the best of men.

EDGAR A. GUEST

A DAD'S GREATEST JOB

I may never be as clever
    as my neighbor down the street.
I may never be as wealthy
    as some other men I meet.
I may never have the glory
    that some other men have had.
But I've got to be successful
    as a little fellow's dad.
There are certain dreams I cherish
    That I'd like to see come true.
There are things I would accomplish
    ere my working time is through.
But the task my heart is set on
    is to guide a little lad
And make myself successful
    as that little fellow's dad.

It's the one job that I dream of,
    It's the task I think of most.
If I fail that growing youngster,
    I'd have nothing else to boast.

91

I may never come to glory.
    I may never gather gold.
Men may count me as a failure
    When my business life is told.
But if he who follows after
    shall be manly, I'll be glad,
For I'll know I've been successful
    as a little fellow's dad.
For though wealth and fame I'd gather
    all my future would be sad,
If I failed to be successful
    as that little fellow's dad.

AUTHOR UNKNOWN

IF WITH PLEASURE YOU ARE VIEWING

If with pleasure you are viewing
Anything your child is doing,
If you like him, if you love him,
Let him know.

Don't withhold appreciation
Until others give expression—
If he wins your commendation
Tell him so.

More than fame and more than money
Is a disposition sunny,
And some hearty warm approval
Makes one glad.

So if you think some praise is due him,
Now's the time to give it to him;
Tie him close with loving language
From his dad.

AUTHOR UNKNOWN

WHAT IS THIS GIFT?

What is this gift you will give your boy?
A glamorous game, a tinseled toy,

A whittling knife, a puzzle pack,
A train that runs on a curving track?
A Boy Scout book, a real live pet?
No, there's plenty of time for such things yet.
Give him a day for his very own—
Just your boy and his dad alone:
A walk in the woods, a game in the park,
A fishing trip from dawn to dark;
Give him the gift to thrill any lad:
The total companionship of his very own dad.
Games are outgrown, and toys decay,
But he'll never forget if you give him a day!

AUTHOR UNKNOWN

YE WHO ARE CALLED TO LABOR

Ye who are called to labor and minister for God,
Blest with the royal priesthood, appointed by his word
To preach among the nations the news of gospel grace,
And publish on the mountains salvation, truth, and peace:

Oh, let not vain ambition nor worldly glory stain
Your minds so pure and holy; acquit yourselves like men.
While lifting up your voices like trumpets long and loud,
Say to the slumb'ring nations: "Prepare to meet your God!"

Then cease from all light speeches, lightmindedness, and pride;
Pray always without ceasing and in the truth abide.
The Comforter will teach you, his richest blessings send.
Your Savior will be with you forever to the end.

Rich blessings there await you, and God will give you faith.
You shall be crowned with glory and triumph over death,
And soon you'll come to Zion, and, bearing each his sheaf,
No more shall taste of sorrow, but glorious crowns receive.

MARY JUDD PAGE

THOUGHTS OF A FATHER

We've never seen the Father here, but we have known the Son,
The finest type of manhood since the world was first begun.

93

And, summing up the works of God, I write with reverent pen,
The greatest is the Son He sent to cheer the lives of men.

Through Him we learned the ways of God and found the Father's
    love;
The Son it was who won us back to Him who reigns above.
The Lord did not come down himself to prove to men His worth,
He sought our worship through the Child He placed upon the earth.

How can I best express my life? Wherein does greatness lie?
How can I long remembrance win, since I am born to die?
Both fame and gold are selfish things; their charms may quickly flee,
But I'm the father of a boy who came to speak for me.

In him lies all I hope to be; his splendor shall be mine;
I shall have done man's greatest work if only he is fine.
If some day he shall help the world long after I am dead,
In all that men shall say of him my praises shall be said.

It matters not what I may win of fleeting gold or fame,
My hope of joy depends alone on what my boy shall claim.
My story must be told through him; for him I work and plan,
Man's greatest duty is to be the father of a man.

EDGAR A. GUEST

Additional poems about fatherhood appear in the topics "Example," "Home and Family," "Teaching," and elsewhere.

FORGIVENESS

TO KNOW ALL IS TO FORGIVE ALL

If I knew you and you knew me—
If both of us could clearly see,
And with an inner sight divine
The meaning of your heart and mine—
I'm sure that we would differ less
And clasp our hands in friendliness;
Our thoughts would pleasantly agree
If I knew you, and you knew me.

NIXON WATERMAN

FORBEARANCE

The kindest and the happiest pair
Will find occasion to forbear;
And something, every day they live,
To pity, and perhaps forgive.

WILLIAM COWPER

THE LAND OF BEGINNING AGAIN

I wish that there were some wonderful place
   In the Land of Beginning Again:
Where all our mistakes and all our heartaches
   And all of our poor selfish grief
Could be dropped like a shabby old coat at the door
   And never put on again.

I wish we could come on it all unaware,
   Like the hunter who finds a lost trail;
And I wish that the one whom our blindness had done
   The greatest injustice of all
Could be there at the gates like an old friend that waits
   For the comrade he's gladdest to hail.

We would find all the things we intended to do
    But forgot, and remembered too late:
Little praises unspoken, little promises broken,
    And all of the thousand and one
Little duties neglected that might have perfected
    The day for one less fortunate.

It wouldn't be possible not to be kind
    In the Land of Beginning Again,
And the ones we misjudged and the ones whom we grudged
    Their moments of victory here,
Would find in the grasp of our loving hand-clasp
    More than penitent lips could explain.

For what had been hardest we'd know had been best,
    And what had seemed loss would be gain;
For there isn't a sting that will not take wing
    When we've faced it and laughed it away;
And I think that the laughter is most what we're after
    In the Land of Beginning Again.

So I wish that there were some wonderful place
    Called the Land of Beginning Again,
Where all our mistakes and all our heartaches
    And all of our poor selfish grief
Could be dropped like a shabby old coat at the door
    And never put on again.

LOUISE FLETCHER TARKINGTON

LET EACH MAN LEARN TO KNOW HIMSELF

Let each man learn to know himself;
To gain this knowledge, let him labor,
Improve those failings in himself
Which he condemns so in his neighbor.
How lenient our own faults we view,
And conscience' voice adroitly smother;
But oh! how harshly we review
The self-same errors in another!

And if you meet an erring one
Whose deeds are blamable or thoughtless,

Consider, ere you cast the stone,
If you yourself be pure and faultless.
Oh! list to that small voice within,
Whose whisperings oft make men confounded,
And trumpet not another's sin,
You'd blush deep if your own were sounded.

And in self-judgment, if you find
Your deeds to others are superior,
To you has Providence been kind,
As you should be to those inferior;
Example sheds a genial ray
Of light which men are apt to borrow;
So, first improve yourself today,
And then improve your friends tomorrow.

AUTHOR UNKNOWN

FORGIVENESS

My heart was heavy, for its trust had been
Abused, its kindness answered with foul wrong;
So, turning gloomily from my fellow-men
One summer Sabbath day I strolled among
The green mounds of the village burial-place;
Where, pondering how all human love and hate
Find one sad level; and how, soon or late,
Wronged and wrongdoer, each with meekened face,
And cold hands folded over a still heart,
Pass the green threshold of our common grave,
Whither all footsteps tend, whence none depart,
Awed for myself, and pitying my race,
Our common sorrow, like a mighty wave,
Swept all my pride away, and trembling I forgave!

JOHN GREENLEAF WHITTIER

EVENING PRAYER

If I have wounded any soul today,
If I have caused one foot to go astray,
If I have walked in my own willful way—
    Good Lord, forgive!

97

If I have uttered idle words or vain,
If I have turned aside from want or pain,
Lest I myself should suffer through the strain—
  Good Lord, forgive!

If I have craved for joys that are not mine,
If I have let my wayward heart repine,
Dwelling on things of earth, not things divine—
  Good Lord, forgive!

If I have been perverse, or hard, or cold,
If I have longed for shelter in Thy fold
When Thou hast given me some part to hold—
  Good Lord, forgive!

Forgive the sins I have confessed to Thee,
Forgive the secret sins I do not see,
That which I know not, Father, teach Thou me—
  Help me to live.

C. MAUD BATTERSBY

*Additional poems about forgiveness appear in the topics "Character,"
"Friendship," "Self-Mastery," and elsewhere.*

FRIENDSHIP

THE ARROW AND THE SONG

I shot an arrow into the air,
It fell to earth, I knew not where;
For, so swiftly it flew, the sight
Could not follow it in its flight.

I breathed a song into the air,
It fell to earth, I knew not where;
For who has sight so keen and strong,
That it can follow the flight of song?

Long, long afterward, in an oak,
I found the arrow, still unbroke;
And the song, from beginning to end,
I found again in the heart of a friend.

HENRY WADSWORTH LONGFELLOW

ALTHOUGH WE TREASURE NEWER FRIENDS

Although we treasure newer friends,
We cannot forget the old.
The new ones are like silver,
The old ones purest gold.

AUTHOR UNKNOWN

PEOPLE LIKED HIM

People liked him, not because
He was rich or known to fame;
He had never won applause
As a star in any game.
His was not a brilliant style;
His was not a forceful way.
But he had a gentle smile
And a kindly word to say.

EDGAR A. GUEST

AROUND THE CORNER

Around the corner I have a friend,
In this great city which has no end;
Yet, days go by and weeks rush on,
And before I know it a year has gone.
And I never see my old friend's face;
For life is a swift and terrible race.
He knows I like him just as well
As in the days when I rang his bell
And he rang mine.

We were younger then
And now we are busy, tired men:
Tired with playing the foolish game;
Tired with trying to make a name;
"Tomorrow," I say, "I will call on Jim,
Just to show I'm thinking of him."
But tomorrow comes and tomorrow goes;
And the distance between us grows and grows

Around the corner! Yet miles away . . .
"Here's a telegram, sir—'Jim died today.'"

And that's what we get—and deserve in the end—
Around the corner, a vanished friend.

CHARLES HANSON TOWNE

A MILE WITH ME

O who will walk a mile with me
   Along life's merry way?
A comrade blithe and full of glee,
Who dares to laugh out loud and free,
And let his frolic fancy play,
Like a happy child, through the flowers gay
That fill the field and fringe the way
   Where he walks a mile with me.

And who will walk a mile with me
   Along life's weary way?

A friend whose heart has eyes to see
The stars shine out o'er the darkening lea,
And the quiet rest at the end o' the day,—
A friend who knows, and dares to say,
The brave, sweet words that cheer the way
    Where he walks a mile with me.

With such a comrade, such a friend,
I fain would walk till journey's end,
Through summer sunshine, winter rain,
And then?—Farewell, we shall meet again!

HENRY VAN DYKE

THE CALL OF LOVE

Far above earth's tumult,
The call of love we hear,
Shall its gentle pleading
Fall on a heedless ear?

O hear the call of love,
O hear the call of love.
The call of love is to mercy
And pardon, and peace,
The call of love is to service
That never shall cease,
Till we shall enter
That land of promise
Where true joys abound,
Then onward press, my comrades,
We are gaining
We are gaining ground.

Not from far off country,
Or land across the sea,
Comes with earnest pleading
The call of love to me.

He who is my neighbor,
And needs a cheering word,
In his faintest whisper
That call of love is heard.

C. AUSTIN MILES

FRIENDSHIP

Oh, the comfort—the inexpressible comfort
    of feeling safe with a person,
Having neither to weigh thoughts,
Nor measure words—but pouring them
All right out—just as they are—
Chaff and grain together—
Certain that a faithful hand will
Take and sift them—
Keep what is worth keeping—
And with the breath of kindness
Blow the rest away.

DINAH MARIA MULOCK CRAIK

THE FRIEND WHO JUST STANDS BY

When trouble comes your soul to try,
You love the friend who just "stands by."
Perhaps there's nothing he can do—
The thing is strictly up to you;
For there are troubles all your own,
And paths the soul must tread alone;
Times when love cannot smooth the road
Nor friendship lift the heavy load,
But just to know you have a friend
Who will "stand by" until the end,
Whose sympathy through all endures,
Whose warm handclasp is always yours—
It helps, someway, to pull you through,
Although there's nothing he can do.
And so with fervent heart you cry,
"God bless the friend who just 'stands by'!"

B. Y. WILLIAMS

ONE SMILE

One smile can glorify the day,
    One word new hope impart;
The least disciple need not say

There are no alms to give away
If love be in the heart.

AUTHOR UNKNOWN

OUTWITTED

He drew a circle that shut me out—
Heretic, rebel, a thing to flout.
But Love and I had the wit to win:
We drew a circle that took him in!

EDWIN MARKHAM

TO A FRIEND

You entered my life in a casual way,
    And saw at a glance what I needed;
There were others who passed me or met me each day,
    But never a one of them heeded.
Perhaps you were thinking of other folks more,
    Or chance simply seemed to decry it;
I know there were many such chances before,
    But the others—well, they didn't see it.

You said just the thing that I wished you would say,
    And you made me believe that you meant it;
I held up my head in the old gallant way,
    And resolved you should never repent it.
There are times when encouragement means such a lot,
    And a word is enough to convey it;
There were others who could have, as easy as not—
    But, just the same, they didn't say it.

There may have been someone who could have done more
    To help me along, though I doubt it;
What I needed was cheering, and always before
    They had let me plod onward without it.
You helped to refashion the dream of my heart,
    And made me turn eagerly to it;
There were others who might have (I question that part)—
    But, after all, they didn't do it!

GRACE STRICKER DAWSON

103

ABOU BEN ADHEM

Abou Ben Adhem (may his tribe increase!)
Awoke one night from a deep dream of peace,
And saw, within the moonlight in his room,
Making it rich, and like a lily in bloom,
An Angel writing in a book of gold:
Exceeding peace had made Ben Adhem bold,
And to the Presence in the room he said,
"What writest thou?" The Vision raised its head,
And with a look made of all sweet accord
Answered, "The names of those who love the Lord."
"And is mine one?" said Abou. "Nay, not so,"
Replied the Angel. Abou spoke more low,
But cheerily still; and said, "I pray thee, then,
Write me as one that loves his fellow men."

The Angel wrote, and vanished. The next night
It came again with a great wakening light,
And showed the names whom love of God had blessed,
And, lo! Ben Adhem's name led all the rest!

LEIGH HUNT

*Additional poems about friendship appear in the topics "Good Works,"
"Love," "Service," and elsewhere.*

GOD

FROM ON ANOTHER'S SORROW

Can I see another's woe,
And not be in sorrow too?
Can I see another's grief,
And not seek for kind relief?

Can I see a falling tear,
And not feel my sorrow's share?
Can a father see his child
Weep, nor be with sorrow fill'd?

Can a mother sit and hear
An infant groan an infant fear?
No, no! never can it be!
Never, never can it be!

And can he who smiles on all
Hear the wren with sorrows small,
Hear the small bird's grief and care,
Hear the woes that infants bear,

And not sit beside the nest,
Pouring pity in their breast;
And not sit the cradle near,
Weeping tear on infant's tear;

And not sit both night and day,
Wiping all our tears away?
O, no! never can it be!
Never, never can it be!

WILLIAM BLAKE

HE GIVETH MORE

He giveth more grace when the burdens grow greater,
    He sendeth more strength when the labors increase;
To added affliction he addeth his mercy,
    To multiplied trials, his multiplied peace.

When we have exhausted our store of endurance,
　　When our strength has failed ere the day is half done,
When we reach the end of our hoarded resources,
　　Our Father's full giving is only begun.

His love has no limit, his grace has no measure,
　　His power no boundary known unto men;
For out of his infinite riches in Jesus
　　He giveth and giveth and giveth again.

ANNIE JOHNSON FLINT

I KNOW NOT WHEN TO GO OR WHERE

　　I know not when I go or where
　　　　From this familiar scene;
　　But He is here and He is there,
　　　　And all the way between;
　　And when I leave this life, I know,
　　　　For that dim vast unknown,
　　Though late I stay, or soon I go,
　　　　I shall not go alone.

AUTHOR UNKNOWN

THOUGH WAVES AND STORMS GO O'ER MY HEAD

Though waves and storms go o'er my head,
　　Though strength, and health and friends be gone,
Though joys be withered all and dead,
　　Though every comfort be withdrawn,
　　　　On this my steadfast soul relies—
　　　　Father, thy mercy never dies!
Fixed on this ground will I remain,
　　Though my heart fail and flesh decay:
This anchor shall my soul sustain,
　　When earth's foundations melt away:
　　　　Mercy's full power I then shall prove,
　　　　Loved with an everlasting love.

JOHN WESLEY

LET NOTHING DISTURB THEE

Let nothing disturb thee,
Nothing affright thee;
All things are passing;
God never changeth:
Patient endurance
Attaineth to all things;
Who God possesseth
In nothing is wanting;
Alone God sufficeth.

HENRY WADSWORTH LONGFELLOW

GOD NEVER FORSOOK AT NEED

God never forsook at need
The soul that trusted Him indeed.

GERALD NEWMARK

FROM THE ETERNAL GOODNESS

O Friends! with whom my feet have trod
  The quiet aisles of prayer,
Glad witness to your zeal for God
  And love of man I bear.

* * *

Ye see the curse which overbroods
  A world of pain and loss;
I hear our Lord's beatitudes
  And prayer upon the cross.

* * *

I see the wrong that round me lies,
  I feel the guilt within;
I hear, with groan and travail-cries,
  The world confess its sin.

Yet, in the maddening maze of things,
  And tossed by storm and flood,
To one fixed trust my spirit clings;
  I know that God is good! . . .

I long for household voices gone,
    For vanished smiles I long,
But God hath led my dear ones on,
    And He can do no wrong.

I know not what the future hath
    Of marvel or surprise,
Assured alone that life and death
    His mercy underlies.

And if my heart and flesh are weak
    To bear an untried pain,
The bruisèd reed He will not break,
    But strengthen and sustain.

* * *

And so beside the Silent Sea
    I wait the muffled oar;
No harm from Him can come to me
    On ocean or on shore.

I know not where his islands lift
    Their fronded palms in air;
I only know I cannot drift
    Beyond his love and care.

JOHN GREENLEAF WHITTIER

OMNIPRESENCE

A thousand sounds, and each a joyful sound;
The dragon flies are humming as they please,
The humming birds are humming all around,
The clithra all alive with buzzing bees,
Each playful lead its separate whisper found,
As laughing winds went rustling through the grove;
And I saw thousands of such sights as these,
And heard a thousand sounds of joy and love.

And yet so dull I was, I did not know
That He was there who all this love displayed,
I did not think how He who loved us so
Shared all my joy, was glad that I was glad;

And all because I did not hear the word
In English accents say, "It is the Lord."

EDWARD EVERETT HALE

HE LEADETH ME

He leadeth me! Oh, blessed thought!
Oh words with heavenly comfort fraught!
Whate'er I do, wher'er I be,
Still 'tis God's hand that leadeth me.

He leadeth me! He leadeth me!
By His own hand He leadeth me;
His faithful follower I would be,
For by His hand He leadeth me.

Sometimes 'mid scenes of deepest gloom,
Sometimes where Eden's bowers bloom,
By waters calm, o'er troubled sea,
Still 'tis God's hand that leadeth me.

Lord, I would clasp Thy hand in mine;
Nor ever murmur nor repine;
Content, whatever lot I see,
Since 'tis God's hand that leadeth me.

And when my task on earth is done,
When, by Thy grace, the victory's won,
E'en death's cold wave I will not flee,
Since Thou through Jordan leadest me.

JOSEPH H. GILMORE

GOD'S HANDWRITING

He writes in characters too grand
For our short sight to understand;
We catch but broken strokes, and try
To fathom all the mystery
Of withered hopes, of death, of life,
The endless war, the useless strife,—

But there, with larger, clearer sight,
We shall see this—

His way was right.

JOHN OXENHAM

Additional poems about God appear in the topics "Faith," "Hope," "Jesus Christ," "Prayer," and elsewhere.

GOOD WORKS

THE COMMON ROAD

I want to travel the common road
With the great crowd surging by,
Where there's many a laugh and many a load,
And many a smile and sigh.
I want to be on the common way
With its endless tramping feet,
In the summer bright and winter gray,
In the noonday sun and heat.
In the cool of evening with shadows nigh,
At dawn, when the sun breaks clear,
I want the great crowd passing by,
To [know] what they see and hear.
I want to be one of the common herd,
Not live in a sheltered way,
Want to be thrilled, want to be stirred
By the great crowd day by day;
To glimpse the restful valleys deep,
To toil up the rugged hill,
To see the brooks which shyly creep,
To have the torrents thrill.
I want to laugh with the common man
Wherever he chance to be,
I want to aid him when I can
Whenever there's need of me.
I want to lend a helping hand
Over the rough and steep
To a child too young to understand—
To comfort those who weep.
I want to live and work and plan
With the great crowd surging by,
To mingle with the common man,
No better or worse than I.

SILAS H. PERKINS

111

BROTHERHOOD

O brother man! fold to thy heart thy brother.
Where pity dwells, the peace of God is there;
To worship rightly is to love each other,
Each smile a hymn, each kindly deed a prayer.

JOHN GREENLEAF WHITTIER

LEND A HAND

I am only one, but I am one;
I can't do everything, but I can do something.
What I can do, that I ought to do;
What I ought to do,
By the grace of God I will do!

EDWARD EVERETT HALE

MY DOOR IS ON THE LATCH

My door is on the latch to-night,
The hearth fire is aglow.
I seem to hear swift passing feet,
The Christ Child in the snow.

My heart is open wide to-night
For stranger, kith or kin.
I would not bar a single door
Where Love might enter in!

KATE DOUGLAS WIGGIN

THE QUALITY OF MERCY

The quality of mercy is not strained,
It droppeth as the gentle rain from heaven
Upon the place beneath. It is twice blessed,
It blesseth him that gives, and him that takes,
'Tis mightiest in the mightiest, it becomes
The throned monarch better than his crown. . . .
It is enthroned in the hearts of kings,
It is an attribute of God himself.

WILLIAM SHAKESPEARE, *THE MERCHANT OF VENICE* 4.1.184–89, 194–95

THE SIN OF OMISSION

It isn't the thing you do;
   It's the thing you leave undone,
Which gives you a bit of heartache
   At the setting of the sun.

The tender word forgotten,
   The letter you did not write,
The flower you might have sent,
   Are your haunting ghosts at night.

The stone you might have lifted
   Out of a brother's way,
The bit of heartsome counsel
   You were hurried too much to say;

The loving touch of the hand,
   The gentle and winsome tone,
That you had no time or thought for
   With troubles enough of your own.

The little acts of kindness,
   So easily out of mind;
Those chances to be helpful
   Which everyone may find—

No, it's not the thing you do,
   It's the thing you leave undone,
Which gives you the bit of heartache
   At the setting of the sun.

MARGARET E. SANGSTER

LOOK UP

Look up and not down.
Look forward and not back.
Look out and not in.
Lend a hand.

EDWARD EVERETT HALE

113

IF YOU CAN SIT AT SET OF SUN

If you can sit at set of sun
And count the deeds that you have done
    And counting find
One self-denying act, one word
That eased the heart of him that heard—
    One glance most kind,
Which fell like sunshine where he went,
Then you may count that day well spent.

But if, thru all the livelong day,
You've cheered no heart, by yea or nay,
    If through it all,
You've nothing done that you can trace
That brought the sunshine to one face—
    No act most small
That helped some soul and nothing cost—
Then count that day as worse than lost.

ROBERT BROWNING

IF I CAN STOP ONE HEART FROM BREAKING

If I can stop one Heart from breaking,
I shall not live in vain;
If I can ease one Life the Aching,
Or cool one pain,
Or help one fainting Robin
Unto his Nest again,
I shall not live in vain.

EMILY DICKINSON

THE PURE, THE BRIGHT, THE BEAUTIFUL

The pure, the bright, the beautiful
    That stirred our hearts in youth,
The impulses to wordless prayer,
    The streams of love and truth,
The longing after something lost,
    The spirit's yearning cry,
The striving after better hopes—
    These things can never die.

The timid hand stretched forth to aid
   A brother in his need;
A kindly word in grief's dark hour
   That proves a friend indeed;
The plea for mercy softly breathed,
   When justice threatens high,
The sorrow of a contrite heart—
   These things shall never die.

Let nothing pass, for every hand
   Must find some work to do,
Lose not a chance to waken love—
   Be firm and just and true.
So shall a light that cannot fade
   Beam on thee from on high,
And angel voices say to thee—
   "These things shall never die."

CHARLES DICKENS

THE HOUSE BY THE SIDE OF THE ROAD

There are hermit souls that live withdrawn
   In the place of their self-content;
There are souls like stars, that dwell apart,
   In a fellowless firmament;
There are pioneer souls that blaze their paths
   Where highways never ran—
But let me live by the side of the road
   And be a friend to man.

Let me live in a house by the side of the road
   Where the race of men go by—
The men who are good and the men who are bad,
   As good and as bad as I.
I would not sit in the scorner's seat
   Or hurl the cynic's ban—
Let me live in a house by the side of the road
   And be a friend to man.

I see from my house by the side of the road,
   By the side of the highway of life,

The men who press with the ardor of hope,
   The men who are faint with the strife,
But I turn not away from their smiles nor their tears.
   Both parts of an infinite plan—
Let me live in a house by the side of the road
   And be a friend to man.

I know there are brook-gladdened meadows ahead,
   And mountains of wearisome height;
That the road passes on through the long afternoon
   And stretches away to the night.
And still I rejoice when the travelers rejoice
   And weep with the strangers that moan,
Nor live in my house by the side of the road
   Like a man who dwells alone.

Let me live in my house by the side of the road,
   It's here the race of men go by—
They are good, they are bad, they are weak, they are strong,
   Wise, foolish—so am I.
Then why should I sit in the scorner's seat,
   Or hurl the cynic's ban?
Let me live in my house by the side of the road
   And be a friend to man.

SAM WALTER FOSS

I HAVE WEPT IN THE NIGHT

I have wept in the night
For the shortness of sight
That to somebody's need made me blind;
But I never have yet
Felt a tinge of regret
For being a little too kind.

AUTHOR UNKNOWN

DO ALL THE GOOD YOU CAN

Do all the good you can,
By all the means you can,
In all the ways you can,

116

In all the places you can,
At all the times you can,
To all the people you can,
As long as ever you can.

JOHN WESLEY

EVERY TASK, HOWEVER SIMPLE

Every task, however simple
    Sets the soul that does it, free;
Every deed of love and mercy
    Done to man, is done to me.

HENRY VAN DYKE

*Additional poems about good works appear in the topics "Character,"
"Example," "Friendship," "Service," and elsewhere.*

GOSSIP AND CRITICISM

THREE GATES

If you are tempted to reveal
A tale to you someone has told
About another, make it pass,
Before you speak, three gates of gold.
These narrow gates: First, "Is it true?"
Then, "Is it needful?" In your mind
Give truthful answer. And the next
Is last and narrowest, "Is it kind?"
And if to reach your lips at last
It passes through these gateways three,
Then you may tell the tale, nor fear
What the result of speech may be.

AUTHOR UNKNOWN

IF YOU KNOW A TALL MAN

If you know a tall man out ahead of the crowd,
A leader of men marching fearless and proud,
And you know a tale which the mere telling aloud
Would cause his proud head in shame to be bowed,
It's a pretty good plan to forget it.

If you know of a skeleton hidden away in a closet,
Guarded and kept from the day in the dark,
Whose showing, whose sudden display,
Would cause grief and sorrow and lifelong dismay,
It's a pretty good plan to forget it.

If you know of a spot in the life of a friend,
We all have such spots concealed world without end,
Which the shame of its telling no grieving could mend,
It's a pretty good thing to forget it.

If you know of a thing that would darken the joy
Of a man or a woman, a girl or a boy,

118

That would sadden or in the least way
Annoy a fellow or cause gladness to stray,
It's a pretty good plan to forget it.

AUTHOR UNKNOWN

BOYS FLYING KITES

Boys flying kites haul in their white-winged birds;
You can call back your kites, but you can't call back your words.
"Careful with fire" is good advice, we know;
"Careful with words" is ten times doubly so.
Thoughts unexpressed will often fall back dead.
But God Himself can't kill them, once they are said!

WILL CARLETON

HEARSAY

In every town, in every street,
In nearly every house, you meet
A little imp, who wriggles in
With half a sneer and half a grin,
And climbs upon your rocking chair,
Or creeps upon you anywhere;
And when he gets you very near,
Just whispers something in your ear—
Some rumor of another's shame—
And "Little Hearsay" is his name.
You understand, this little elf
He doesn't say he knows himself,
He doesn't claim it's really true—
He only whispers it to you,
Because he knows you'll go and tell
Some other whisperer as well.
And if he says he's only heard,
Declare you don't believe a word,
And tell him you will not repeat
The silly chatter of the street.
However gossips smile and smirk,
Refuse to do their devil's work.

AUTHOR UNKNOWN

119

YOU NEVER CAN TELL

You never can tell when you send a word
    Like an arrow shot from a bow
By an archer blind, be it cruel or kind,
    Just where it may chance to go.
It may pierce the breast of your dearest friend,
    Tipped with its poison or balm,
To a stranger's heart in life's great mart
    It may carry its pain or its calm.

You never can tell when you do an act
    Just what the result will be,
But with every deed you are sowing a seed,
    Though the harvest you may not see.
Each kindly act is an acorn dropped
    In God's productive soil;
You may not know, but the tree shall grow
    With shelter for those who toil.

You never can tell what your thoughts will do
    In bringing you hate or love,
For thoughts are things, and their airy wings
    Are swifter than carrier doves.
They follow the law of the universe—
    Each thing must create its kind,
And they speed o'er the track to bring you back
    Whatever went out from your mind.

ELLA WHEELER WILCOX

THREE THINGS COME NOT BACK

Remember three things come not back:
The arrow sent upon its track—
It will not swerve, it will not stay
Its speed; it flies to wound, or slay.
The spoken word so soon forgot
By thee; but it has perished not;
In other hearts 'tis living still
And doing work for good or ill.
And the lost opportunity
That cometh back no more to thee,

120

In vain thou sweepest, in vain dost yearn,
Those three will nevermore return.

AUTHOR UNKNOWN

SHOULD YOU FEEL INCLINED TO CENSURE

Should you feel inclined to censure
Faults you may in others view,
Ask your own heart, ere you venture,
If you have not failings, too.
Let not friendly vows be broken;
Rather strive a friend to gain.
Many words in anger spoken
Find their passage home again.

Do not, then, in idle pleasure
Trifle with a brother's fame;
Guard it as a valued treasure,
Sacred as your own good name.
Do not form opinions blindly;
Hastiness to trouble tends;
Those of whom we thought unkindly
Oft become our warmest friends.

AUTHOR UNKNOWN

LET SOMETHING GOOD BE SAID

When over the fair fame of friend or foe
    The shadow of disgrace shall fall, instead
Of words of blame, or proof of thus and so,
    Let something good be said.

Forget not that no fellow-being yet
    May fall so low but love may lift his head:
Even the cheek of shame with tears is wet,
    If something good be said.

No generous heart may vainly turn aside
    In ways of sympathy; no soul so dead
But may awaken strong and glorified,
    If something good be said.

121

And so I charge ye, by the thorny crown,
   And by the cross on which the Saviour bled,
And by your own soul's hope of fair renown,
   Let something good be said!

JAMES WHITCOMB RILEY

ON FILE

If an unkind word appears,
   File the thing away.
If some novelty in jeers,
   File the thing away.
If some clever little bit
Of a sharp and pointed wit,
Carrying a sting with it—
   File the thing away.

If some bit of gossip come,
   File the thing away.
Scandalously spicy crumb,
   File the thing away.
If suspicion comes to you
That your neighbor isn't true
Let me tell you what to do—
   File the thing away.

Do this for a little while,
Then go out and burn the file.

JOHN KENDRICK BANGS

A WISE OLD OWL

A wise old owl lived in an oak;
The more he saw the less he spoke;
The less he spoke the more he heard:
Why can't we all be like that bird?

AUTHOR UNKNOWN

I KNOW SOMETHING GOOD ABOUT YOU

Wouldn't this old world be better,
If the folks we meet would say—
"I know something good about you!"
And treat us just that way?

Wouldn't it be fine and dandy
If each handclasp, fond and true,
Carried with it this assurance—
"I know something good about you!"

Wouldn't life be lots more happy
If the good that's in us all
Were the only thing about us
That folks bothered to recall?

Wouldn't life be lots more happy
If we praised the good we see?
For there's such a lot of goodness
In the worst of you and me!

Wouldn't it be nice to practice
That fine way of thinking, too?
You know something good about me,
I know something good about you.

AUTHOR UNKNOWN

Additional poems about gossip and criticism appear in the topics "Friendship," "Judging," "Love," and elsewhere.

GRATITUDE

I WANDERED LONELY AS A CLOUD

I wandered lonely as a cloud
That floats on high o'er vales and hills,
When all at once I saw a crowd,
A host, of golden daffodils,
Beside the lake, beneath the trees,
Fluttering and dancing in the breeze.

Continuous as the stars that shine
And twinkle on the milky way,
They stretched in never-ending line
Along the margin of a bay;
Ten thousand saw I at a glance
Tossing their heads in sprightly dance.

The waves beside them danced, but they
Outdid the sparkling waves in glee;
A poet could not but be gay,
In such a jocund company;
I gazed—and gazed—but little thought
What wealth the show to me had brought:

For oft, when on my couch I lie
In vacant or in pensive mood,
They flash upon that inward eye
Which is the bliss of solitude;
And then my heart with pleasure fills,
And dances with the daffodils.

WILLIAM WORDSWORTH

GRATITUDE

O God! We give our thanks to thee,
For thy redeeming love for us,
Thy loving watch, on land or sea,
For all that's grand and glorious.

The verdant vales and mountains high,
And songsters in the leafy bowers,
For sun and moon, and starlit sky,
The fragrance of a thousand flowers.

We thank thee for the gospel's light
To guide us mortals here below,
The snow-clad peaks, so pure and white,
From which the crystal waters flow.
For thy protecting care and love
And all the good we hear and see:
For all thy blessings from above,
We give, Oh God, our thanks to thee.

JOSEPH D. OLSON

PRAISE TO THE LORD, THE ALMIGHTY

Praise to the Lord, the Almighty, the King of creation!
O my soul, praise him, for he is thy health and salvation!
Join the great throng,
Psaltery, organ, and song,
Sounding in glad adoration!

Praise to the Lord! Over all things he gloriously reigneth.
Borne as on eagle wings, safely his Saints he sustaineth.
Hast thou not seen
How all thou needest hath been
Granted in what he ordaineth?

Praise to the Lord, who doth prosper thy way and defend thee.
Surely his goodness and mercy shall ever attend thee.
Ponder anew
What the Almighty can do,
Who with his love doth befriend thee.

Praise to the Lord! Oh, let all that is in me adore him!
All that hath breath, join with Abraham's seed to adore him!
Let the "amen"
Sum all our praises again,
Now as we worship before him.

JOACHIM NEANDER

OH, GOD, I THANK THEE

Oh, God, I thank thee for each sight
Of beauty that thy world doth give.
For sunny sky and air and light,
Oh, God, I thank thee that I live.

That life I consecrate to thee
And ever as the day is born
On wings of joy my soul doth flee
And thank thee for another morn.

Another morn in which to cast
Some silent deed of love abroad,
That great'ning as it journeys past
May do some earnest work for God.

AUTHOR UNKNOWN

THE WORLD IS MINE!

Today upon a bus I saw a lovely maid with golden hair;
I envied her—she seemed so gay—and I wished I were as fair.
When suddenly she rose to leave, I saw her hobble down the aisle;
She had one foot and wore a crutch, but as she passed, a smile.
Oh, God, forgive me when I whine.
I have two feet; the world is mine!

And then I stopped to buy some sweets.
The lad who sold them had such charm.
I talked with him; he said to me,
"It's nice to talk with folks like you.
You see," he said, "I'm blind."
Oh, God, forgive me when I whine.
I have two eyes; the world is mine!

Then walking down the street,
I saw a child with eyes of blue.
He stood and watched the others play;
It seemed he knew not what to do.
I stopped for a moment, then I said,
"Why don't you join the others, dear?"

He looked ahead without a word,
And then I knew he could not hear.
Oh, God, forgive me when I whine.
I have two ears; the world is mine!

With feet to take me where I'd go,
With eyes to see the sunset's glow,
With ears to hear what I would know,
Oh, God, forgive me when I whine.
I'm blessed, indeed! The world is mine!

AUTHOR UNKNOWN

HOW SHARPER THAN A SERPENT'S TOOTH

How sharper than a serpent's tooth it is
To have a thankless child!

WILLIAM SHAKESPEARE, *KING LEAR*, 1.4.310–11

NO LONGER FORWARD

No longer forward nor behind
    I look in hope or fear;
But grateful, take the good I find
    The best of now and here.

JOHN GREENLEAF WHITTIER

FROM A LITTLE TE DEUM OF THE COMMONPLACE

For all things beautiful, and good, and true;
For things that seemed not good yet turned to good;
For all the sweet compulsions of Thy will
That chastened, tried, and wrought us to Thy shape;
For things unnumbered that we take of right,
And value first when they are withheld;
For light and air; sweet sense of sound and smell;
For ears to hear the heavenly harmonies;
For eyes to see the unseen in the seen;
For vision of the Worker in the work;
For hearts to apprehend Thee everywhere;—
We thank Thee, Lord!

JOHN OXENHAM

THE UNDISCOVERED COUNTRY

Lord, for the erring thought
Not unto evil wrought:
Lord, for the wicked will
Betrayed and baffled still:
For the heart from itself kept,
Our thanksgiving accept.
For ignorant hopes that were
Broken to our blind prayer:
For pain, death, sorrow sent
Unto our chastisement:
For all loss of seeming good,
Quicken our gratitude.

WILLIAM DEAN HOWELLS

FOR SUNLIT HOURS

For sunlit hours and visions clear,
For all remembered faces dear,
For comrades of a single day,
Who sent us stronger on our way,
For friends who shared the year's long road,
And bore with us the common load,
For hours that levied heavy tolls,
But brought us nearer to our goals,
For insights won through toil and tears,
We thank the Keeper of our years.

CLYDE McGEE

*Additional poems about gratitude appear in the topics "Happiness,"
"Humility," "Thanksgiving," and elsewhere.*

HAPPINESS

LITTLE THINGS

Little drops of water,
Little grains of sand,
Make the mighty ocean
And the pleasant land. . . .

Little deeds of kindness,
Little words of love,
Help to make earth happy
Like the heaven above.

JULIA FLETCHER CARNEY

THE DOOR OF HAPPINESS

All wondering and eager-eyed,
    Within her portico,
I made my plea of Hostess Life,
    One morning long ago.
"Pray, show me this great house of thine,
    Nor close a single door,

For many rooms and curious things
    And treasures great and small
Within this spacious mansion lie,
    And I would see them all."
Then Hostess Life turned silently
    Her searching gaze on me,
And with no word she reached her hand,
    And offered up the key.

It opened first the Door of Hope,
    And long I lingered there,
Until I spied the Room of Dreams,
    Just higher by a stair,

And then a door, whereon the word
   "Happiness" was writ,
But when I tried the little key,
   I could not make it fit.

It unlocked the door of "Pleasure's Room,"
   Where ev'rything seemed so bright,
But after I had stayed a while,
   It somehow lost its light;
And wandering down the little hall,
   I came upon a room
Marked "Duty," and entered it
   To find myself in gloom.

Along its shadowy walls I groped
   My weary way about,
And found that from dull Duty's Room
   The door of Toil led out.
It led out into another room,
   Whereon a crimson stain
Marked sullenly against the dark
   The words "The Room of Pain."

But oh! the light, the light, the light!
   That spilled down from above!
And upward wound the stairs of Faith,
   Right to the Tower of Love.
And when I came forth from that place,
   I tried the little key,
And lo! the Door of Happiness
   Swung open wide and free.

AUTHOR UNKNOWN

O HEART OF MINE, WE SHOULDN'T WORRY SO!

O heart of mine, we shouldn't
   Worry so!
What we've missed of calm we couldn't
   Have, you know!
What we've met of stormy pain,
And of sorrow's driving rain,
We can better meet again,
   If it blow!

We have erred in that dark hour
   We have known,
When our tears fell with the shower,
   All alone!—
Were not shine and shower blent
As the gracious Master meant?—
Let us temper our content
   With His own.

For, we know, not every morrow
   Can be sad;
So, forgetting all the sorrow
   We have had,
Let us fold away our fears,
And put by our foolish tears,
And through all the coming years
   Just be glad.

JAMES WHITCOMB RILEY

MATINS

Flowers rejoice when night is done,
Lift their heads to greet the sun;
Sweetest looks and odours raise,
In a silent hymn of praise.

So my heart would turn away
From the darkness to the day;
Lying open in God's sight
Like a flower in the light.

HENRY VAN DYKE

EPIGRAM ON HIS FAMILY ARMS

Live while you live, the epicure would say,
And seize the pleasures of the present day;
Live while you live, the sacred preacher cries,
And give to God each moment as it flies.
Lord, in my view let both united be;
I live in pleasure when I live to Thee.

PHILIP DODDRIDGE

THESE ARE THE GIFTS I ASK

These are the gifts I ask of Thee,
    Spirit serene:
Strength for the daily task,
Courage to face the road,
Good cheer to help me bear the traveler's load,
    And, for the hours of rest that come between,
An inward joy of all things heard and seen.

HENRY VAN DYKE

WHEN LIFE SEEMS JUST A DREARY GRIND

When life seems just a dreary grind,
    And things seem fated to annoy,
Say something nice to someone else
    And watch the world light up with joy.

AUTHOR UNKNOWN

SOLITUDE

Laugh and the world laughs with you,
    Weep and you weep alone;
For the sad old earth must borrow its mirth,
    But has troubles enough of its own.

ELLA WHEELER WILCOX

HOW HAPPY IS THE LITTLE STONE

How happy is the little stone
That rambles in the road alone,
And doesn't care about careers,
And exigencies never fears;
Whose coat of elemental brown
A passing Universe put on;
And independent as the sun,
Associates or glows alone,
Fulfilling absolute decree
In casual simplicity.

EMILY DICKINSON

SUNSHINE AND MUSIC

A laugh is just like sunshine.
It freshens all the day,
It tips the peak of life with light,
And drives the clouds away.
The soul grows glad that hears it
And feels its courage strong.
A laugh is just like sunshine
For cheering folks along.

A laugh is just like music.
It lingers in the heart,
And where its melody is heard
The ills of life depart;
And happy thoughts come crowding
Its joyful notes to greet:
A laugh is just like music
For making living sweet.

AUTHOR UNKNOWN

OUT IN THE FIELDS WITH GOD

The little cares that fretted me,
    I lost them yesterday
Among the fields above the sea,
    Among the winds at play;
Among the lowing of the herds,
    The rustling of the trees,
Among the singing of the birds,
    The humming of the bees.

The foolish fears of what may happen
    I cast them all away
Among the clover-scented grass,
    Among the new-mown hay;
Among the husking of the corn
    Where drowsy poppies nod,
Where ill thoughts die and good are born,
    Out in the fields with God.

ELIZABETH BARRETT BROWNING

MY CROWN IS IN MY HEART

My crown is in my heart, not on my head;
Not deck'd with diamonds and Indian stones,
Nor to be seen: my crown is call'd content;
A crown it is that seldom kings enjoy.

WILLIAM SHAKESPEARE, *KING HENRY VI* 3.3.1.62–65

CLOUDS AND SUNSHINE

The way at times may dark and dreary seem,
No ray of sunshine on our path may beam,
The dark clouds hover o'er us like a pall,
And gloom and sadness seem to compass all,
But still with honest purpose toil we on;
And if our course be upright, firm and true,
Far in the east, the golden light shall dawn
And the bright smile of God come bursting through.

AUTHOR UNKNOWN

Additional poems about happiness appear in the topics "Character," "Friendship," "Home and Family," and elsewhere.

HOME AND FAMILY

MORNING PRAYER

When little things would irk me, and I grow
Impatient with my dear one, make me know
How in a moment joy can take its flight
And happiness be quenched in endless night.
Keep this thought with me all the livelong day
That I may guard the harsh words I might say
When I would fret and grumble, fiery hot,
At trifles that tomorrow are forgot—
Let me remember, Lord, how it would be
If these, my loved ones, were not here with me.

ELLA WHEELER WILCOX

STAY, STAY AT HOME

Stay, stay at home, my heart, and rest;
Home-keeping hearts are happiest,
For those that wander they know not where
Are full of trouble and full of care;
    To stay at home is best.

Weary and homesick and distressed,
They wander east, they wander west,
And are baffled and beaten and blown about
By the winds of the wilderness of doubt;
    To stay at home is best.

Then stay at home, my heart, and rest;
The bird is safest in its nest,
Over all that flutter their wings and fly
A hawk is hovering in the sky;
    To stay at home is best.

HENRY WADSWORTH LONGFELLOW

WE ARE ALL HERE!

We are all here!
Father, mother, sister, brother,
All who hold each other dear.
Each chair is filled—
We're all at home. . . .
We're all—all here.

AUTHOR UNKNOWN

TOGETHER

You and I by this lamp with these
Few books shut out the world. Our knees
Touch almost in this little space.
But I am glad. I see your face.
The silences are long, but each
Hears the other without speech.
And in this simple scene there is
The essence of all subtleties,
The freedom from all fret and smart,
The one sure sabbath of the heart.

The world—we cannot conquer it,
Nor change the minds of fools one whit.
Here, here alone do we create
Beauty and peace inviolate;
Here night by night and hour by hour
We build a high impregnable tower
Whence may shine, now and again,
A light to light the feet of men
When they see the rays thereof:
And this is marriage, this is love.

LUDWIG LEWISOHN

BEFORE IT IS TOO LATE

If you have a tender message,
    Or a loving word to say,
Do not wait till you forget it,
    But whisper it today;

136

The tender word unspoken,
    The letter never sent,
The long forgotten messages,
    The wealth of love unspent—
For these some hearts are breaking,
    For these some loved ones wait;
So show them that you care for them
    Before it is too late.

Frank Herbert Sweet

'MID PLEASURES AND PALACES

'Mid pleasures and palaces though we may roam,
Be it ever so humble, there's no place like home;
A charm from the sky seems to hallow us there,
Which, seek through the world, is ne'er met with elsewhere.

An exile from home, splendor dazzles in vain;
Oh, give me my lowly thatched cottage again!
The birds singing gaily, that came at my call—
Give me them—and the peace of mind, dearer than all!

I gaze on the moon as I tread the drear wild,
And feel that my mother now thinks of her child,
As she looks on that moon from our own cottage door
Thro' the woodbine, whose fragrance shall cheer me no more.

How sweet 'tis to sit 'neath a fond father's smile,
And the caress of a mother to soothe and beguile!
Let others delight 'mid new pleasure to roam,
But give me, oh, give me, the pleasures of home,

To thee I'll return, overburdened with care;
The heart's dearest solace will smile on me there;
No more from that cottage again will I roam;
Be it ever so humble, there's no place like home.
Home, home, sweet, sweet home!
There's no place like home, oh, there's no place like home!

John Howard Payne

MY WIFE

Helping and loving and guiding,
Urging when that were best,
Watching and guarding, whispering still,
Win you can—and you must, you will!

AUTHOR UNKNOWN

WHERE IS MY WANDERING BOY TONIGHT?

Where is my wandering boy tonight?
   The boy of my tend'rest care:
The boy that was once my joy and light,
   The child of my love and prayer.

Once he was pure as the morning dew,
   As he knelt at his mother's knee;
No face was so bright, no heart more true,
   And none was as sweet as he.

Oh, could I see him now, my boy,
   As fair as in olden time,
When prattle and smile made home a joy,
   And life was a merry chime.

Go, for my wandering boy tonight,
   Go search for him where you will:
But bring him to me with all his blight,
   and tell him I love him still.
Oh, where is my boy tonight?
   Where is my boy tonight?
My heart o'erflows, for I love him, he knows,
   Oh, where is my boy tonight?

AUTHOR UNKNOWN

NO PLACE TO GO

The happiest nights
   I ever know
Are those when I've
   No place to go,

138

And the missus says
    When the day is through:
"To-night we haven't
    A thing to do."

Oh, the joy of it,
    And the peace untold
Of sitting 'round
    In my slippers old,
With my [favorite] book
    In my easy chair,
Knowing I needn't
    Go anywhere.

Needn't hurry
    My evening meal
Nor force the smiles
    That I do not feel,
But can grab a book
    From a near-by shelf,
And drop all sham
    And be myself.

Oh, the joy of it,
    Oh, the comfort rare,
Nothing on this earth
    To it can compare.
And I'm sorry for him
    Who doesn't know
The joy of having
    No place to go.

EDGAR A. GUEST

WE NEED NOT POWER

We need not power or splendor,
Wide halls, or lordly dome;
The good, the true, the tender—
These form the wealth of home.

AUTHOR UNKNOWN

SO LONG AS THERE ARE HOMES

So long as there are homes to which men turn at close of day;
So long as there are homes where children are, where women stay—
If love and loyalty and faith be found across those sills—
A stricken nation can recover from its gravest ills.

So long as there are homes where fires burn and there is bread;
So long as there are homes where lamps are lit and prayers are said;
Although a people falter through the dark—and nations grope,
With God Himself back of these little homes, we have sure hope.

AUTHOR UNKNOWN

FROM WHICH SHALL IT BE?

"Which shall it be? Which shall it be?"
I looked at John, John looked at me,
And when I found that I must speak,
My voice seemed strangely low and weak:
"Tell me again what Robert said,"
And then I, listening, bent my head.
"This is his letter: 'I will give
A house and land while you shall live,
If, in return, from out your seven,
One child to me forever is given.'"

I looked at John's old garments worn;
I thought of all that he had borne
Of poverty, and work, and care,
Which I, though willing, could not share;
I thought of seven young mouths to feed,
Of seven little children's need,
And then of this. "Come, John," said I,
"We'll choose among them as they lie
Asleep." So, walking hand in hand,
Dear John and I surveyed our band.
First to the cradle lightly stepped,
Where the new nameless baby slept.
"Shall it be Baby?" whispered John.
I took his hand, and hurried on
To Lily's crib. Her father lay
His rough hand down in a loving way,

140

When dream or whisper made her stir,
And huskily he said: "Not her!"

We stooped beside the trundle bed,
And one long ray of lamplight shed
Athwart the boyish faces there,
In sleep so beautiful and fair;
I saw on Jamie's rough, red cheek
A tear undried. E'er John could speak,
"He's but a baby, too," said I,
And kissed him as we hurried by.
Pale, patient, Robbie's angel face
Still in his sleep bore suffering's trace.
"No, for a thousand crowns, not him!"
We whispered, while our eyes were dim.

Poor Dick! bad Dick! our wayward son—
Turbulent, restless, idle one—
Could he be spared? Nay, He who gave
Bade us befriend him to the grave;
Only a mother's heart could be
Patient enough for such as he;
"And so," said John, "I would not dare
To send him from her bedside prayer."

Then stole we softly up above,
And knelt by Mary, child of love.
"Perhaps for her 'twould better be,"
I said to John. Quite silently
He lifted up a curl that lay
Across her cheek in a wilful way,
And shook his head: "Nay, love, not thee,"
The while my heart beat audibly.

Only one more, our eldest lad,
Trusty and truthful, good and glad,
So like his father. "No, John, no!
I cannot, will not, let him go."

And so we wrote, in courteous way,
We could not give one child away;
And afterward toil lighter seemed,
Thinking of that of which we dreamed,

Happy in truth that not one face
Was missed from its accustomed place;
Thankful to work for all the seven,
Trusting the rest to One in heaven.

ETHEL LYNN BEERS, ADAPTED

PRAYER OF PARENTHOOD

I thank Thee, Oh God, for being,
For *what,* and for *why* I am;
For wedded companionship without end;
For a life blended with lives that through me come—
Help me, O God, to know these lives as they are:
To companion them each day and hour,
to live before them that faith that carries on, and on—even toward
    divinity.
That mine may be that joy unutterable—
A sweet, uplifting presence to each life through mine,
And unto Thee be all praise forever. Amen.

AUTHOR UNKNOWN

IF THERE IS RIGHTEOUSNESS

If there is righteousness in the heart,
    There will be beauty in the character.
If there is beauty in the character,
    There will be harmony in the home.
If there is harmony in the home,
    There will be order in the nation.
If there is order in the nation,
    There will be peace in the world.

AUTHOR UNKNOWN

A HOUSE IS BUILT OF STICKS

A house is built of sticks and stones
    and tiles and posts and piers,
But a home is built of loving deeds
    that stand a thousand years.

VICTOR HUGO

142

THE STICK-TOGETHER FAMILIES

The stick-together families are happier by far
Than the brothers and the sisters who take separate highways are.
The gladdest people living are the wholesome folks who make
A circle at the fireside that no power but death can break.
And the finest of conventions ever held beneath the sun
Are the little family gatherings when the busy day is done.

There are rich folk, there are poor folk, who imagine they are wise,
And they're very quick to shatter all the little family ties.
Each goes searching after pleasure in his own selected way,
Each with strangers likes to wander, and with strangers likes to play.
But it's bitterness they harvest, and it's empty joy they find,
For the children that are wisest are the stick-together kind.

There are some who seem to fancy that for gladness they must roam,
That for smiles that are the brightest they must wander far from
    home.
That the strange friend is the true friend, and they travel far astray
And they waste their lives in striving for a joy that's far away,
But the gladdest sort of people, when the busy day is done,
Are the brothers and the sisters who together share their fun.

It's the stick-together family that wins the joys of earth,
That hears the sweetest music and that finds the finest mirth;
It's the old home roof that shelters all the charm that life can give;
There you find the gladdest play-ground, there the happiest spot to live.
And, O weary, wandering brother, if contentment you would win,
Come you back unto the fireside and be comrade with your kin.

EDGAR A. GUEST

THERE ARE THREE WORDS

There are three words that sweetly blend,
That on the heart are graven;
A precious, soothing balm they lend:
They're mother, home and heaven.

AUTHOR UNKNOWN

*Additional poems about home and family appear in the topics "Fatherhood,"
"Love," "Motherhood," and elsewhere.*

HOPE

HOPE

Hope, like a gleaming taper's light,
  Adorns and cheers our way;
And still, as darker grows the night,
  Emits a brighter ray.

OLIVER GOLDSMITH

HE HAD HIS DREAM

He had his dream, and all through life,
Worked up to it through toil and strife.
Afloat fore'er before his eyes,
It colored for him all his skies:
    The storm-cloud dark
    Above his bark,
The calm and listless vault of blue
Took on its hopeful hue,
It tinctured every passing beam—
    He had his dream.

He labored hard and failed at last,
His sails too weak to bear the blast,
The raging tempests tore away
And sent his beating bark astray.
    But what cared he
    For wind or sea!
He said, "The tempest will be short,
My bark will come to port."
He saw through every cloud a gleam—
    He had his dream.

PAUL LAURENCE DUNBAR

A NEW EARTH

God grant us wisdom in these coming days,
  And eyes unsealed, that we clear visions see

144

Of that new world that He would have us build,
　　To life's ennoblement and His high ministry.

God give us sense—God-sense of life's new needs,
　　And souls aflame with new-born chivalries—
To cope with those black growths that foul the ways,—
　　To cleanse our poisoned founts with God-born energies.

To pledge our souls to nobler, loftier life,
　　To win the world to His fair sanctities,
To bind the nations in a pact of peace,
　　And free the soul of life for finer loyalties.

Not since Christ died upon His lonely cross
　　Has time such prospect held of life's new birth;
Not since the world of chaos first was born
　　Has man so clearly visaged hope of a new earth.

Not of our own might can we hope to rise
　　Above the ruts and soilures of the past,
But, with His help who did the first earth build,
　　With hearts courageous we may fairer build this last.

JOHN OXENHAM

LIFE'S LESSONS

I learn, as the years roll onward
　　And leave the past behind,
That much I had counted sorrow
　　But proves that God is kind;
That many a flower I had longed for
　　Had hidden a thorn of pain,
And many a rugged bypath
　　Led to fields of ripened grain.

The clouds that cover the sunshine
　　They can not banish the sun;
And the earth shines out the brighter
　　When the weary rain is done.
We must stand in the deepest shadow
　　To see the clearest light;
And often through wrong's own darkness
　　Comes the very strength of light.

The sweetest rest is at even,
    After a wearisome day,
When the heavy burden of labor
    Has borne from our hearts away;
And those who have never known sorrow
    Can not know the infinite peace
That falls on the troubled spirit
    When it sees at last release.

We must live through the dreary winter
    If we would value the spring;
And the woods must be cold and silent
    Before the robins sing.
The flowers must be buried in darkness
    Before they can bud and bloom,
And the sweetest, warmest sunshine
    Comes after the storm and gloom.

AUTHOR UNKNOWN

MY GRANDAD

My grandad, viewing earth's worn cogs,
Said things are going to the dogs.
His grandad in his house of logs,
Said things are going to the dogs.
His grandad in the Flemish bogs,
Said things are going to the dogs.
His grandad in his old skin togs,
Said things are going to the dogs.
There's one thing I have to state:
The dogs have had a good long wait!

AUTHOR UNKNOWN

THE LARGER TRUST
FROM *IN MEMORIAM*

O yet we trust that somehow good
Will be the final goal of ill,

* * *

That nothing walks with aimless feet,
That not one life shall be destroyed

146

Or cast as rubbish to the void,
When God hath made the pile complete;

That not a worm is cloven in vain;
That not a moth with vain desire
Is shriveled in a fruitless fire,
But subserves another's gain.

Behold, we know not anything;
I can but trust that good will fall
At last—far off—at last, to all,
And every winter change to spring.

ALFRED, LORD TENNYSON

UNDER THE STORM AND THE CLOUD

Under the storm and the cloud today,
    And today the hard peril and pain,
Tomorrow the stone shall be rolled away,
    For the sunshine shall follow the rain.
Merciful Father, I will not complain,
I know that the sunshine shall follow the rain.

AUTHOR UNKNOWN

THE LOST CHORD

Seated one day at the Organ,
    I was weary and ill at ease,
And my fingers wandered idly
    Over the noisy keys.

I know not what I was playing,
    Or what I was dreaming then;
But I struck one chord of music,
    Like the sound of a great Amen.

It flooded the crimson twilight,
    Like the close of an angel's Psalm,
And it lay on my fevered spirit
    With a touch of infinite calm.

147

It quieted pain and sorrow,
   Like love overcoming strife;
It seemed the harmonious echo
   From our discordant life.

It linked all perplexed meanings
   Into one perfect peace,
And trembled away into silence
   As if it were loth to cease.

I have sought but I seek it vainly,
   That one lost chord divine,
Which came from the soul of the Organ
   And entered into mine.

It may be that Death's bright angel
   Will speak in that chord again—
It may be that only in Heaven
   I shall hear that great Amen.

ADELAIDE ANNE PROCTER

FAREWELL, LIFE
WRITTEN DURING SICKNESS

Farewell, life! my senses swim,
And the world is growing dim;
Thronging shadows cloud the light,
Like the advent of the night,—
Colder, colder, colder still,
Upward steals a vapor chill;
Strong the earthly odor grows,—
I smell the mould above the rose!

Welcome, life! the spirit strives!
Strength returns and hope revives;
Cloudy fears and shapes forlorn
Fly like shadows at the morn,—
O'er the earth there comes a bloom;
Sunny light for sullen gloom,
Warm perfume for vapor cold,—
I smell the rose above the mould!

THOMAS HOOD

TO THE FRINGED GENTIAN

Thou blossom, bright with autumn dew,
And colored with the heaven's own blue,
That openest when the quiet light
Succeeds the keen and frosty night;

Thou comest not when violets lean
O'er wandering brooks and springs unseen,
Or columbines, in purple dressed,
Nod o'er the ground-bird's hidden nest.

Thou waitest late, and com'st alone,
When woods are bare and birds are flown,
And frosts and shortening days are portend
The aged Year is near his end.

Then doth thy sweet and quiet eye
Look through its fringes to the sky,
Blue—blue—as if that sky let fall
A flower from its cerulean wall.

I would that thus, when I shall see
The hour of death draw near to me,
Hope, blossoming within my heart,
May look to heaven as I depart.

WILLIAM CULLEN BRYANT

THE GOAL

I care not that the storm sways all the trees,
    And floods the plain and blinds my trusting sight;
I only care that o'er the land and seas
    Comes somewhere Love's perpetual peace and light.

I care not that sharp thorns grow thick below,
    And wound my hands and scar my anxious feet;
I only care to know God's roses grow,
    And I may somewhere find their odor sweet.

I care not if they be not white, but red,
    Red as the blood-drops from a wounded heart;

I only care to ease my aching head
  With faith that somewhere God hath done His part.

I care not if, in years of such despair,
  I reach in vain and seize no purpose vast;
I only care that I sometime, somewhere,
  May find a meaning, shining at the last.

Frank Wakely Gunsaulus

Additional poems about hope appear in the topics "Courage," "Faith," and elsewhere.

HUMILITY AND PRIDE

THE SHEPHERD BOY'S SONG

He that is down need fear no fall,
    He that is low, no pride;
He that is humble, ever shall
    Have God to be his guide.
I am content with what I have,
    Little be it, or much:
And, Lord, contentment still I crave,
    Because thou savest such.
Fulness to such, a burden is,
    That go on pilgrimage;
Here little, and hereafter bliss,
    Is best from age to age.

JOHN BUNYAN

FROM RECESSIONAL

God of our fathers, known of old,
Lord of our far-flung battle-line,
Beneath whose awful Hand we hold
Dominion over palm and pine—
Lord God of Hosts, be with us yet,
Lest we forget—lest we forget!

The tumult and the shouting dies;
The Captains and the Kings depart:
Still stands Thine ancient sacrifice,
An humble and a contrite heart.
Lord God of Hosts, be with us yet,
Lest we forget—lest we forget!

Far called, our navies melt away;
On dune and head-land sinks the fire:
Lo, all our pomp of yesterday
Is one with Nineveh and Tyre!
Judge of the Nations, spare us yet,
Lest we forget—lest we forget!

RUDYARD KIPLING

OZYMANDIAS

I met a traveller from an antique land
Who said: Two vast and trunkless legs of stone
Stand in the desert. Near them, on the sand,
Half sunk, a shattered visage lies, whose frown,
And wrinkled lip, and sneer of cold command,
Tell that its sculptor well those passions read
Which yet survive, stamped on these lifeless things,
The hand that mocked them, and the heart that fed:
And on the pedestal these words appear:
"My name is Ozymandias, king of kings:
Look on my works, ye Mighty, and despair!"
Nothing beside remains. Round the decay
Of that colossal wreck, boundless and bare
The lone and level sands stretch far away.

PERCY BYSSHE SHELLEY

"FATHER, WHERE SHALL I WORK TODAY?"

"Father, where shall I work today?"
And my love flowed warm and free.
Then he pointed out a tiny spot
And said, "Tend that for me."
I answered quickly, "Oh no, not that!
Why, no one would ever see,
No matter how well my work was done.
Not that little place for me."
And the word he spoke, it was not stern;
He answered me tenderly:
"Ah, little one, search that heart of thine;
Art thou working for them or for me?
Nazareth was a little place,
And so was Galilee."

MEADE MacGUIRE

PRAYER

Father, I scarcely dare to pray,
    So clear I see, now it is done,

152

That I have wasted half my day,
　And left my work but just begun.

So clear I see that things I thought
　Were right or harmless were a sin;
So clear I see that I have sought,
　Unconscious, selfish aims to win.

So clear I see that I have hurt
　The souls I might have helped to save;
That I have slothful been, inert,
　Deaf to the calls Thy leaders gave.

In outskirts of Thy kingdom vast,
　Father, the humblest spot give me;
Set me the lowliest task Thou hast;
　Let me, repentant, work for Thee!

HELEN HUNT JACKSON

THE HAPPIEST HEART

Who drives the horse of the sun
　Shall lord it but a day.
Better the lowly deed were done
　And kept the humble way.

The rust will find the sword of fame;
　The dust will hide the crowd,
Aye, none shall nail so high his name
　Time will not tear it down.

The happiest heart that ever beat
　Was in some quiet breast
That found the common daylight sweet
　And left to heaven the rest.

JOHN VANCE CHENEY

THE LOWEST PLACE

Give me the lowest place, not that I dare
　Ask for that lowest place, but Thou hast died

153

That I might live and share
   Thy glory by Thy side.

Give me the lowest place; or if for me
   That lowest place too high, make one more low
Where I may sit and see
   My God and love Thee so.

CHRISTINA ROSSETTI

THE SIMPLE THINGS

I would not be too wise—so very wise
   That I must sneer at simple songs and creeds,
And let the glare of wisdom blind my eyes
   To humble people and their humble needs.

I would not care to climb so high that I
   Could never hear the children at their play,
Could only see the people passing by,
   And never hear the cheering words they say.

I would not know too much—too much to smile
   At trivial errors of the heart and hand,
Nor be too proud to play the friend the while.
   Nor cease to help and know and understand.

I would not care to sit upon a throne,
   Or build my house upon a mountain-top,
Where I must dwell in glory all alone
   And never friend come in or poor man stop.

God grant that I may live upon this earth
   And face the tasks which every morning brings
And never lose the glory and the worth
   Of humble service and the simple things.

EDGAR A. GUEST

TRUE GREATNESS

That man is great, and he alone,
Who serves a greatness not his own,

154

For neither praise nor pelf:
Content to know and be unknown:
Whole in himself.

OWEN MEREDITH, LORD BULWER-LYTTON

TWO WENT UP TO THE TEMPLE TO PRAY

Two went to pray? O, rather say,
One went to brag, the other to pray;

One stands up close and treads on high,
Where the other dares not lend his eye;

One nearer to God's altar trod,
The other to the altar's God.

RICHARD CRASHAW

*Additional poems about humility and pride appear in the topics "Character,"
"Courage," "Integrity," and elsewhere.*

INDIVIDUAL WORTH

WHERE DID YOU COME FROM?

Where did you come from, Baby dear?
Out of the everywhere into here.

Where did you get your eyes so blue?
Out of the sky as I came through.

What makes the light in them sparkle and spin?
Some of the starry spikes left in.

Where did you get that little tear?
I found it waiting when I got here.

What makes your forehead so smooth and high?
A soft hand stroked it as I went by.

What makes your cheek like a warm white rose?
I saw something better than anyone knows.

Whence that three-corner'd smile of bliss?
Three angels gave me at once a kiss.

Where did you get this pearly ear?
God spoke, and it came out to hear. . . .

How did they all come just to be you?
God thought of me, and so I grew.

But how did you come to us, you dear?
God thought of you, and so I am here.

GEORGE MACDONALD

TOUCHING SHOULDERS

There's a comforting thought at the close of the day,
When I'm weary and lonely and sad,
That sort of grips hold of my crusty old heart
And bids it be merry and glad.

156

It gets in my soul and it drives out the blues,
And finally thrills through and through.
It is just a sweet memory that chants the refrain:
"I'm glad I touch shoulders with you!"

Did you know you were brave, did you know you were strong?
Did you know there was one leaning hard?
Did you know that I waited and listened and prayed,
And was cheered by your simplest word?
Did you know that I longed for that smile on your face,
For the sound of your voice ringing true?
Did you know I grew stronger and better because
I had merely touched shoulders with you?

I am glad that I live, that I battle and strive
For the place that I know I must fill;
I am thankful for sorrows, I'll meet with a grin
What fortune may send, good or ill.
I may not have wealth, I may not be great,
But I know I shall always be true,
For I have in my life that courage you gave
When once I rubbed shoulders with you.

AUTHOR UNKNOWN

BEAUTIFUL THINGS

Beautiful faces are those that wear—
It matters little if dark or fair—
Whole-souled honesty printed there.

Beautiful eyes are those that show,
Like crystal panes where hearthfires glow,
Beautiful thoughts that burn below.

Beautiful lips are those whose words
Leap from the heart like songs of birds,
Yet whose utterance prudence girds.

Beautiful hands are those that do
Work that is honest and brave and true,
Moment by moment the long day through.

157

Beautiful feet are those that go
On kindly ministries to and fro,
Down lowliest ways, if God wills it so.

Beautiful shoulders are those that bear
Ceaseless burdens of homely care
With patient grace and daily prayer.

Beautiful lives are those that bless
Silent rivers of happiness,
Whose hidden fountains but few may guess.

Beautiful twilight at set of sun,
Beautiful goal with race well won,
Beautiful rest with work well done.

Beautiful graves where grasses creep,
Where brown leaves fall, where drifts lie deep
Over worn-out hands—oh! beautiful sleep!

ELLEN P. ALLERTON

REWARD

Who does God's work will get God's pay,
However long may seem the day,
However weary be the way.
No mortal hand God's hand can stay;
He may not pay as others pay,
In gold, or lands, or raiment gay,
In goods that perish and decay;
But God's high wisdom knows a way,
And this is sure, let come what may—
Who does God's work will get God's pay.

AUTHOR UNKNOWN

TRUE WORTH

True worth is being, not seeming;
In doing each day that goes by
Some little good—not in the dreaming
Of great things to do by-and-by.

158

For whatever men say in blindness,
   And spite of the fancies of youth,
There's nothing so kingly as kindness,
   And nothing so royal as truth.

ALICE CARY

WEIGHING THE BABY

How many pounds does the baby weigh—
   Baby who came but a month ago?
How many pounds from the crowning curl
   To the rosy point of the restless toe?

Grandfather ties the 'kerchief knot,
   Tenderly guides the swinging weight,
And carefully over his glasses peers
   To read the record: "Only eight."

Softly the echo goes around:
   The father laughs at the tiny girl;
The fair young mother sings the words,
   While grandmother smooths the golden curl.

And stooping above the precious thing,
   Nestles a kiss, within a prayer.
Murmuring softly, "Little one,
   Grandfather didn't weigh you fair."

Nobody weighed the baby's smile,
   Or the love that came with the helpless one;
Nobody weighed the threads of care,
   From which a woman's life is spun.

Nobody weighed the baby's soul
   For here on earth, no weights there be
That would avail. God only knows
   Its value in eternity.

ETHEL LYNN BEERS

Additional poems about individual worth appear in the topics "Character," "Divine Nature," "Integrity," and elsewhere.

INTEGRITY

THE MAN IN THE GLASS

When you get what you want in your struggle for self
And the world thinks you king for a day,
Just go to the mirror and look at yourself,
And see what *that* man has to say.

For it isn't your father, your mother, or wife
Who judgment upon you must pass;
The fellow whose verdict counts most in your life
Is the one staring back from the glass.

You may be like Jack Horner and chisel a plum
And think you're a wonderful guy;
But the man in the glass says you're only a bum
If you can't look him straight in the eye.

He's the fellow to please, never mind all the rest;
For he's with you clear to the end.
And you've passed your most dangerous, difficult test
If the man in the glass is your friend.

You may fool the whole world down the pathway of years
And get pats on the back as you pass;
But your final reward will be heartaches and tears
If you've cheated the man in the glass.

AUTHOR UNKNOWN

GOOD NAME

Good name in man or woman, dear my lord,
Is the immediate jewel of their souls.
Who steals my purse steals trash—'tis something, nothing,
'Twas mine, 'tis his, and has been slave to thousands;
But he that filches from me my good name
Robs me of that which not enriches him
And makes me poor indeed.

WILLIAM SHAKESPEARE, *OTHELLO* 3.3.155–61

160

A REAL MAN

Men are of two kinds, and he
Was of the kind I'd like to be.
Some preach their virtues, and a few
Express their lives by what they do.
That sort was he. No flowery phrase
Or glibly spoken words of praise
Won friends for him. He wasn't cheap
Or shallow, but his course ran deep,
And it was pure. You know the kind.
Not many in a life you find
Whose deeds outrun their words so far
That more than what they seem they are.

There are two kinds of lies as well:
The kind you live, the ones you tell.
Back through his years from age to youth
He never acted one untruth.
Out in the open light he fought
And didn't care what others thought
Nor what they said about his fight
If he believed that he was right.
The only deeds he ever hid
Were acts of kindness that he did.

What speech he had was plain and blunt.
His was an unattractive front.
Yet children loved him; babe and boy
Played with the strength he could employ,
Without one fear, and they are fleet
To sense injustice and deceit.
No back door gossip linked his name
With any shady tale of shame.
He did not have to compromise
With evil-doers, shrewd and wise,
And let them ply their vicious trade
Because of some past escapade.

Men are of two kinds, and he
Was of the kind I'd like to be.

No door at which he ever knocked
Against his manly form was locked.
If ever man on earth was free
And independent, it was he.
No broken pledge lost him respect,
He met all men with head erect,
And when he passed I think there went
A soul to yonder firmament
So white, so splendid and so fine
It came almost to God's design.

EDGAR A. GUEST

MY NAME IS LEGION

Within my earthly temple there's a crowd;
There's one of us that's humble, one that's proud,
There's one that's broken-hearted for his sins,
There's one that unrepentant sits and grins;
There's one that loves his neighbor as himself,
And one that cares for naught but fame and pelf.
From much corroding care I should be free
If I could once determine which is me!

EDWARD SANFORD MARTIN

GOD GRANT ME THIS

God grant me this: the right to come at night
Back to my loved ones, head erect and true;
Beaten and bruised and from a losing fight,
Let me be proud in what I've tried to do.

Let me come home defeated if I must,
But clean of hands, and honor unimpaired,
Still holding firmly to my children's trust,
Still worthy of the faith which they have shared.

God grant me this: what e'er the fates decree,
Or do I win or lose life's little game,
I still would keep my children proud of me,
Nor once regret that they must bear my name.

EDGAR A. GUEST

162

IF I WERE A VOICE

If I were a voice, a persuasive voice,
That could travel the wide world through,
I would fly on the beams of the morning light,
And speak to men with a gentle might,
And tell them to be true.

I'd fly o'er land and sea,
Wherever a human heart might be,
Telling a tale, or singing a song,
In praise of the Right and in blame of the Wrong.

CHARLES MACKAY

TO THINE OWN SELF BE TRUE

To thine own self be true,
And it must follow, as the night the day,
Thou canst not then be false to any man.

WILLIAM SHAKESPEARE, *HAMLET* 1.3.78–80

YOU OUGHT TO BE FINE

You ought to be fine for the sake of the folks
    Who think you are fine.
If others have faith in you doubly you're bound
    To stick to the line.
It's not only on you that dishonor descends:
You can't hurt yourself without hurting your friends.

You ought to be true for the sake of the folks
    Who believe you are true.
You never should stoop to a deed that your friends
    Think you wouldn't do.
If you're false to yourself, be the blemish but small,
You have injured your friends; you've been false to them all.

For friendship, my boy, is a bond between men
    That is founded on truth;
It believes in the best of the ones that it loves,
    Whether old man or youth;

And the stern rule it lays down for me and for you
Is to be what our friends think we are, through and through.

AUTHOR UNKNOWN

A HEART UNTAINTED

What stronger breastplate than a heart untainted!
Thrice is he arm'd that hath his quarrel just,
And he but naked, though locked up in steel,
Whose conscience with injustice is corrupted.

WILLIAM SHAKESPEARE, KING HENRY VI 2.3.2.232–35

Additional poems about integrity appear in the topics "Character," "Courage," "Example," "Self-Mastery," and elsewhere.

JESUS CHRIST

THE PEACE-GIVER

Thou whose birth on earth
  Angels sang to men,
While Thy stars made mirth,
Saviour, at Thy birth,
  This day born again;

As this night was bright
  With Thy cradle-ray,
Very Light of Light,
Turn the wild world's night
  To Thy perfect day.

Thou the Word and Lord
  In all time and space
Heard, beheld, adored,
With all ages poured
  Forth before Thy face,

Lord, what worth in earth
  Drew Thee down to die?
What therein was worth,
Lord, Thy death and birth?
  What beneath Thy sky?

Thou whose face gives grace
  As the sun's doth heat,
Let Thy sunbright face
Lighten time and space
  Here beneath Thy feet.

Bid our peace increase,
  Thou that madest morn;
Bid oppression cease;
Bid the night be peace;
  Bid the day be born.

ALGERNON CHARLES SWINBURNE

WHAT CAN I GIVE HIM?

What can I give Him,
Poor as I am?
If I were a shepherd
I would bring a lamb.
If I were a Wise Man
I would do my part,
Yet what can I give Him?
Give my heart.

CHRISTINA ROSSETTI

LOVE DIVINE, ALL LOVE EXCELLING

Love divine, all love excelling,
    Joy of heav'n to earth come down!
Fix in us Thy humble dwelling;
    All Thy faithful mercies crown.
Jesus, Thou art all compassion,
    Pure unbounded love Thou art;
Visit us with Thy salvation;
    Enter every trusting heart.

JOHN WESLEY

THO' CHRIST A THOUSAND TIMES BE BORN

Tho' Christ a thousand times in Bethlehem be born,
If He's not born in thee, thy soul is still forlorn.

JOHANNES SCHEFFLER

THE LAMB
FROM SONGS OF INNOCENCE

Little Lamb, who made thee?
Dost thou know who made thee?
Gave thee life, and bid thee feed
By the stream and o'er the mead;
Gave thee clothing of delight,
Softest clothing, woolly, bright;
Gave thee such a tender voice,
Making all the vales rejoice?

Little Lamb, I'll tell thee,
Little Lamb, I'll tell thee,
He is called by thy name,
For he calls himself a Lamb;
He is meek, and he is mild;
He became a little child.
I a child, and thou a lamb,
We are called by his name.
Little Lamb, God bless thee!
Little Lamb, God bless thee!

WILLIAM BLAKE

A CHILD'S OFFERING

The wise may bring their learning,
    The rich may bring their wealth,
And some may bring their greatness,
    And some bring strength and health;
We, too, would bring our treasures
    To offer to the King;
We have no wealth or learning:
    What shall we children bring?

We'll bring Him hearts that love Him;
    We'll bring Him thankful praise,
And young souls meekly striving
    To walk in holy ways:
And these shall be the treasures
    We offer to the King,
And these are gifts that even
    The poorest child may bring.

We'll bring the little duties
    We have to do each day;
We'll try our best to please Him,
    At home, at school, at play:
And better are these treasures
    To offer to our King,
Than richest gifts without them;
    Yet these a child may bring.

AUTHOR UNKNOWN

HOW SIMPLE

How simple we must grow!
How simple they who came!
The shepherds looked at God
Long before any man.
He sees God nevermore
Not there, nor here on earth
Who does not long within
To be a shepherd first.

ANGELUS SILESIUS

I THINK WHEN I READ THAT SWEET STORY

I think when I read that sweet story of old,
When Jesus was here among men,
How he called little children like lambs to his fold;
I should like to have been with him then.

I wish that his hands had been placed on my head,
That his arms had been thrown around me,
That I might have seen his kind look when he said,
"Let the little ones come unto me."

JEMIMA LUKE

MY MASTER

My Master was so very poor,
A manger was His cradling place;
So very rich my Master was
Kings came from far
To gain His grace.

My Master was so very poor
And with the poor He broke the bread;
So very rich my Master was
That multitudes
By Him were fed.

My Master was so very poor
They nailed Him naked to a cross;
So very rich my Master was

He gave His all
And knew no loss.

HARRY LEE

IN THE GARDEN

My sins, my sins, my Savior!
  Their guilt I never knew
Till with thee in the desert
  I near thy passion drew;
Till with thee in the garden
  I heard thy pleading prayer,
And saw the sweat-drops bloody
  That told thy sorrow there.

J. B. S. MONSELL

HIS HANDS

The hands of Christ
  Seem very frail,
For they were broken
  By a nail.

But only they reach
  Heaven at last
Whom these frail, broken
  Hands hold fast.

JOHN RICHARD MORELAND

TO THIS END

And hast Thou help for such as me,
Sin-weary, stained, forlorn?
  "Yea then,—if not for such as thee
  To what end was I born?"

But I have strayed so far away,
So oft forgotten Thee.
  "No smallest thing that thou hast done
  But was all known to Me."

169

And I have followed other gods,
And brought Thy name to scorn.
 "It was to win thee back from them
  I wore the crown of thorn."

And, spite of all, Thou canst forgive,
And still attend my cry?
 "Dear heart, for this end I did live,
  To this end did I die."

And if I fall away again,
And bring Thy Love to shame?
 "I'll find thee out where'er thou art,
  And still thy love will claim."

All this for me, whose constant lack
Doth cause Thee constant pain?
 "For this I lived, for this I died,
  For this I live again."

JOHN OXENHAM

FAIREST LORD JESUS

 Fairest Lord Jesus
 Ruler of all nature
O thou of God and man the Son!
 Thee will I cherish,
 Thee will I honor,
Thou my soul's glory, joy and crown.

 Fair are the meadows,
 Fairer still the woodlands,
Robed in the blooming garb of spring;
 Jesus is fairer,
 Jesus is purer,
Who makes the woeful heart to sing.

 Fair is the sunshine,
 Fairer still the moonlight,
And all the twinkling, starry host;

Jesus shines fairer,
Jesus shines purer,
Than all the angels heaven can boast.

AUTHOR UNKNOWN, TWELFTH CENTURY

KILLED IN ACTION

"Killed in action . . . in the line of duty."
Blind went her eyes with pain. . . .
A moan of mortal agony,
Then all became still again.

"Oh God! . . . my God! . . . where were you
When my son was being slain?"
And the scalding tears of bitterness
Drenched her cheeks like the summer rain.

But a soft voice seemed to whisper
In the twilight's afterglow,
"I had a son . . . at Calvary . . .
Two thousand years ago."

AUTHOR UNKNOWN

LOVE SO AMAZING, SO DIVINE

When I survey the wondrous cross
On which the Prince of glory died,
My richest gain I count but loss,
And pour contempt on all my pride.

Forbid it, Lord, that I should boast,
Save in the death of Christ, my God!
All the vain things that charm me most,
I sacrifice them to his blood. . . .

Were the whole realm of nature mine,
That were a present far too small;
Love, so amazing, so divine,
Demands my soul, my life, my all!

ISAAC WATTS

IN HIS STEPS

The road is rough, I said,
   Dear Lord, there are stones that hurt me so.
And he said, Dear child, I understand,
   I walked it long ago.

But there is a cool green path, I said,
   Let me walk there for a time.
No child, He gently answered me,
   The green road does not climb.

My burden, I said, is far too great;
   How can I bear it so?
My child, said he, I remember weight.
   I carried my cross, you know.

But, I said, I wish there were friends with me
   Who would make my way their own.
Ah, yes, he said, Gethsemane
   Was hard to face alone.

And so I climbed the stony path,
   Content at last to know
That where my Master had not gone
   I would not need to go.

And strangely then I found new friends;
The burden grew less sore
As I remembered—long ago
   He went that way before.

LEONA B. GATES

I'VE FOUND A FRIEND

I've found a friend, oh, such a friend,
So kind, and true, and tender,
So wise a counselor and guide,
So mighty a defender.

I've found a friend, oh, such a friend.
He bled, he died to save me,

172

And not alone the gift of life,
But his own self he gave me.

I've found a friend, oh, such a friend.
All power to him is given
To guide me on my onward course
And bring me safe to heaven.

J. G. SMALL

COME, THOU FOUNT OF EVERY BLESSING

Come, thou Fount of every blessing;
Tune my heart to sing thy grace;
Streams of mercy, never ceasing,
Call for songs of loudest praise.
Teach me some melodious sonnet,
Sung by flaming tongues above;
Praise the mount; I'm fixed upon it:
Mount of thy redeeming love.

O to grace how great a debtor
Daily I'm constrained to be!
Let thy goodness, as a fetter,
Bind my wandering heart to thee.
Prone to wander, Lord, I feel it,
Prone to leave the God I love;
Here's my heart, O take and seal it;
Seal it for thy courts above.

ROBERT ROBINSON

THE KING OF LOVE

The King of love my Shepherd is,
    Whose goodness faileth never;
I nothing lack if I am His,
    And He is mine forever.

Where streams of living water flow
    My ransomed soul He leadeth,
And where the verdant pastures grow
    With food celestial feedeth.

173

Perverse and foolish oft I strayed,
    But yet in love He sought me,
And on His shoulder gently laid,
    And home rejoicing brought me.

In death's dark vale I fear no ill,
    With Thee, dear Lord, beside me;
Thy rod and staff my comfort still,
    Thy life before to guide me.

Thou spread'st a table in my sight;
    Thy suff'ring grace bestoweth;
And O what transport of delight
    From Thy pure chalice floweth.

And so, through all the length of day,
    Thy goodness faileth never;
Good Shepherd, may I sing Thy praise
    Within Thy house forever.

HENRY W. BAKER

FROM THE VISION OF SIR LAUNFAL

"Lo, it is I, be not afraid!
In many climes, without avail,
Thou hast spent thy life for the Holy Grail;
Behold, it is here—this cup which thou
Didst fill at the streamlet for me but now;
This crust is my body broken for thee,
The water his blood that died on the tree;
The holy supper is kept, indeed,
In whatso we share with another's need;
Not what we give, but what we share,
For the gift without the giver is bare;
Who gives himself with his alms feeds three—
Himself, his hungering neighbor, and Me."

JAMES RUSSELL LOWELL

HIS GRACE IS GREAT ENOUGH

His grace is great enough to meet the great things—
    The crashing waves that overwhelm the soul,
The roaring winds that leave us stunned and breathless,
    The sudden storms beyond our life's control.

His grace is great enough to meet the small things—
    The little pin-prick troubles that annoy,
The insect worries, buzzing and persistent,
    The squeaking wheels that grate upon our joy.

ANNIE JOHNSON FLINT

THE TOUCH OF THE MASTER'S HAND

'Twas battered and scarred, and the auctioneer
Thought it scarcely worth his while
To waste much time on the old violin,
But held it up with a smile:
"What am I bidden, good folks," he cried,
"Who'll start the bidding for me?"
"A dollar, a dollar"; then, "Two!" "Only two?
Two dollars, and who'll make it three?
Three dollars, once; three dollars, twice;
Going for three—" But no,
From the room, far back, a gray-haired man
Came forward and picked up the bow;
Then, wiping the dust from the old violin,
And tightening the loose strings,
He played a melody pure and sweet
As a caroling angel sings.

The music ceased, and the auctioneer,
With a voice that was quiet and low,
Said, "What am I bid for the old violin?"
And he held it up with the bow.
"A thousand dollars, and who'll make it two?
Two thousand! And who'll make it three?
Three thousand, once, three thousand, twice,
And going, and gone!" said he.
The people cheered, but some of them cried,
"We do not quite understand

What changed its worth." Swift came the reply:
"The touch of a master's hand."

And many a man with life out of tune,
And battered and scarred with sin,
Is auctioned cheap to the thoughtless crowd,
Much like the old violin.
A "mess of pottage," a glass of wine,
A game—and he travels on.
He's "going" once, and "going" twice,
He's "going" and almost "gone."
But the Master comes, and the foolish crowd
Never can quite understand
The worth of a soul and the change that's wrought
By the touch of the Master's hand.

MYRA BROOKS WELCH

THE PRINCE OF PEACE

The Prince of Peace His banner spreads,
His wayward folk to lead
From war's embattled hates and dreads,
Its bulwarked ire and greed.
O marshal us, the sons of sires
Who braved the cannon's roar,
To venture all that peace requires
As they dared death for war.

Lead on, O Christ! That haunting song
No centuries can dim,
Which long ago the heavenly throng
Sang over Bethlehem.
Cast down our rancor, fear, and pride,
Exalt goodwill again!
Our worship doth Thy name deride,
Bring we not peace to men.

Thy pardon, Lord, for war's dark shame,
Its death-strewn, bloody fields!
Yet thanks to Thee for souls aflame
Who dared with swords and shields;
O Christ, who died to give men life,

Bring that victorious hour,
When man shall use for peace, not strife,
His valor, skill, and power.

Cleanse all our hearts from our disgrace—
We love not world, but clan!
Make clear our eyes to see our race
One family of man.
Rend Thou our little temple veils
That cloak the truth divine,
Until Thy mighty word prevails,
That cries, "All souls are mine."

HARRY EMERSON FOSDICK

THE COMING OF THE LORD

Come suddenly, O Lord, or slowly come:
I wait thy will; thy servant ready is:
Thou hast prepared thy follower a home,—
The heaven in which thou dwellest, too, is his.

Come in the morn, at noon, or midnight deep;
Come, for thy servant still doth watch and pray:
E'en when the world around is sunk in sleep,
I wake and long to see thy glorious day.

I would not fix the time, the day, nor hour,
When thou with all thine angels shalt appear;
When in thy kingdom thou shalt come with power,—
E'en now, perhaps, the promised day is near!

For though in slumber deep the world may lie,
And [even some] forget thy great command;
Still, year by year, thy coming draweth nigh,
And in its power thy kingdom is at hand.

Not in some future world alone 't will be,
Beyond the grave, beyond the bounds of time;
But on the earth thy glory we shall see,
And share thy triumph, peaceful, pure, sublime.

Lord, help me that I faint not, weary grow,
Nor at thy coming slumber, too, and sleep;
For thou hast promised, and full well I know
Thou wilt to us thy word of promise keep.

JONES VERY

Additional poems about Jesus Christ appear in the topics "Christmas," "Death and Immortality," "Easter," "Example," "God," "Service," and elsewhere.

JUDGING

IF I HAD KNOWN

If I had known what trouble you were bearing;
What griefs were in the silence of your face;
I would have been more gentle, and more caring,
And tried to give you gladness for a space.
I would have brought more warmth into the place,
   If I had known.

If I had known what thoughts despairing drew you;
(Why do we never try to understand?)
I would have lent a little friendship to you,
And slipped my hand within your hand,
And made your stay more pleasant in the land,
   If I had known.

MARY CAROLYN DAVIES

A PLEA FOR THOSE WHO ERR

Think gently of the erring one;
   O let us not forget,
However darkly stained by sin,
   He is our brother yet.

Heir of the same inheritance,
   Child of the selfsame God,
He hath but stumbled in the path
   We have in weakness trod.

Speak gently to the erring ones;
   We yet may lead them back,
With holy words, and tones of love,
   From misery's thorny track.

Forget not, brother, thou hast sinned,
   And sinful yet mayst be;
Deal gently with the erring heart,
   As God has dealt with thee.

HENRY A. TUCKETT

MEN MAY MISJUDGE THY AIM

Men may misjudge thy aim,
Think they have cause to blame,
Say thou art wrong;
Keep on thy quiet way,
Christ is the Judge, not they,
Fear not; be strong.

AUTHOR UNKNOWN

WHEN YOU GET TO KNOW A FELLOW

When you get to know a fellow, know his joys and know his cares,
When you've come to understand him and the burdens that he bears,
When you've learned the fight he's making and the troubles in his
way,
Then you find that he is different than you thought him yesterday.
Then you will find his faults are trivial and there's not so much to
blame
In the brother that you jeered at when you only knew his name.

You are quick to see the blemish in the distant neighbor's style,
You can point to all his errors and may sneer at him the while,
And your prejudices fatten and your hates more violent grow
As you talk about the failure of the man you do not know,
But when drawn a little closer, and your hands and shoulders touch,
You find the traits you hated really don't amount to much.

When you get to know a fellow, know his every mood and whim,
You begin to find the texture of the splendid side of him;
You begin to understand him, and you cease to scoff and sneer,
For with understanding always prejudices disappear.
You begin to find his virtues and his faults you cease to tell,
For you seldom hate a fellow when you know him very well.

When next you start in sneering and your phrases turn to blame,
Know more of him you censure than his business and his name;
For it's likely that acquaintance would your prejudice dispel
And you'd really come to like him if you knew him very well.
Then his faults won't really matter, for you'll find a lot to praise.
When you get to know a fellow and you understand his ways.

EDGAR A. GUEST

BROKEN FRIENDSHIP

Alas! they had been friends in youth,
But whispering tongues can poison truth!
And constancy lives in realms above!
And life is thorny, and Youth is vain!
And to be wroth with one we love,
Doth work like madness in the brain!
They parted—ne'er to meet again!
But never either found another
To free the hollow heart from paining!
They stood aloof, the scars remaining;
Like cliffs which had been rent asunder!
A dreary sea now flows between;
But neither heat, nor frost, nor thunder,
Shall wholly do away, I ween,
The marks of that which once had been.

SAMUEL TAYLOR COLERIDGE

RETRIBUTION

Though the mills of God grind slowly,
Yet they grind exceeding small;
Though with patience He stands waiting,
With exactness grinds He all.

FRIEDRICH VON LOGAU

JUDGE NOT

Pray do not find fault with the man
Who limps, or stumbles along the road
Unless you've worn the shoes he wears
Or struggled beneath his load.
There may be tacks in him that hurt
Though hidden away from view,
Or the burden placed on your back
Might cause you to stumble too.
Unless you've felt the blow
That caused his fall, or felt the shame

181

That only he can know.
You may be strong, but still the blows
That were his, if dealt to you
In selfsame way and selfsame time
Might cause you to stagger too.
Don't be too harsh with him who sins
Or pelt him with word or stone
Unless you're sure, yea, doubly sure
That you've no sins of your own.
For you know, perhaps if tempter's voice
Should whisper soft to you,
As it did to him that went astray,
'Twould cause you to falter too.

AUTHOR UNKNOWN

NOT UNDERSTOOD

Not understood. We move along asunder,
    Our paths grow wider as the seasons creep
Along the years; we marvel and we wonder
    Why life is life, and then we fall asleep,
        Not understood.

Not understood. We gather false impressions
    And hug them closer as the years go by,
Till virtues often seem to us transgressions;
    And thus men rise and fall and live and die,
        Not understood.

Not understood. Poor souls with stunted vision
    Oft measure giants by their narrow gauge.
The poisoned shafts of falsehood and derision
    Are oft impelled 'gainst those who mould the age,
        Not understood.

Not understood. The secret springs of action,
    Which lie beneath the surface and the show,
Are disregarded; with self-satisfaction
    We judge our neighbors as they often go,
        Not understood.

Not understood. How trifles often change us.
    The thoughtless sentence or the fancied slight
Destroys long years of friendships, and estranges us,
    And on our souls there falls a freezing blight:
        Not understood.

Not understood. How many breasts are aching,
    For lack of sympathy? Ah! day to day,
How many cheerless, lonely hearts are breaking!
    How many noble spirits pass away,
        Not understood.

O God, that men would see a little clearer,
    Or judge less harshly where they cannot see!
O God, that men would draw a little nearer
    To one another! They'd be nearer Thee
        And understood.

THOMAS BRACKEN

SO MUCH GOOD

There is so much good in the worst of us,
And so much bad in the best of us,
That it hardly behooves any of us
To talk about the rest of us.

AUTHOR UNKNOWN

Additional poems about judging appear in the topics "Friendship," "Gossip and Criticism," and elsewhere.

KNOWLEDGE AND WISDOM

HE WHO KNOWS NOT

He who knows not and knows not that he knows not
    Is a fool—shun him.
He who knows not and knows that he knows not
    Is simple—teach him.
He who knows and knows not that he knows
    Is asleep—awaken him.
He who knows and knows that he knows
    Is wise—follow him.

PERSIAN PROVERB

THOUGHTS

You never can tell what thoughts will do
In bringing you hate or love,
For thoughts are things
With their airy wings
That are swifter than carrier dove.
They follow the law of the universe:
Each thing must create its kind;
And they sweep o'er the track
To bring you back
Whatever went out from your mind.

AUTHOR UNKNOWN

AT TWENTY

At twenty I knew, and I knew I knew—
    While at thirty, I wasn't sure.
At forty I knew that I didn't know
    A lot I had known before.
At fifty I sigh, and wonder how
    One who had known so much so young,
Can know so little now.

DAPHNE JEMMETT

LORD OF THE FAR HORIZONS

Lord of the far horizons,
    Give us the eyes to see
Over the verge of sundown
    The beauty that is to be.
Give us the skill to fashion
    The task of Thy command,
Eager to follow the pattern
    We may not understand.

Master of ancient wisdom
    And the lore lost long ago,
Inspire our foolish reason
    With faith to seek and know.
When the skein of truth is tangled,
    And the lead of sense is blind,
Foster the fire to lighten
    Our unillumined mind.

BLISS CARMAN

THE BLIND MEN AND THE ELEPHANT

It was six men of Indostan
    To learning much inclined,
Who went to see the elephant
    (Though all of them were blind),
That each by observation
    Might satisfy his mind.

The First approached the elephant,
    And, happening to fall
Against his broad and sturdy side,
    At once began to bawl:
"God bless me! but the elephant
    Is nothing but a wall!"

The Second, feeling of the tusk,
    Cried: "Ho! what have we here
So very round and smooth and sharp?
    To me 'tis mighty clear

185

This wonder of an elephant
　Is very like a spear!"

The Third approached the animal,
　And, happening to take
The squirming trunk within his hands,
　Thus boldly up and spake:
"I see," quoth he, "the elephant
　Is very like a snake!"

The Fourth reached out his eager hand,
　And felt about the knee:
"What most this wondrous beast is like
　Is mighty plain," quoth he;
"'Tis clear enough the elephant
　Is very like a tree."

The Fifth, who chanced to touch the ear,
　Said: "E'en the blindest man
Can tell what this resembles most;
　Deny the fact who can,
This marvel of an elephant
　Is very like a fan!"

The Sixth no sooner had begun
　About the beast to grope,
Than, seizing on the swinging tail
　That fell within his scope,
"I see," quoth he, "the elephant
　Is very like a rope!"

And so these men of Indostan
　Disputed loud and long,
Each in his own opinion
　Exceeding stiff and strong,
Though each was partly in the right,
　And all were in the wrong!

So, oft in theologic wars
　The disputants, I ween,
Rail on in utter ignorance
　Of what each other mean,

And prate about an elephant
Not one of them has seen!

JOHN GODFREY SAXE

WISDOM
FROM *THE TASK*

Knowledge and wisdom, far from being one,
Have oft times no connection. Knowledge dwells
In heads replete with thoughts of other men:
Wisdom in minds attentive to their own.
Knowledge is proud that he has learn'd so much;
Wisdom is humble that he knows no more.

WILLIAM COWPER

BOOKS ARE KEYS

Books are keys to wisdom's treasure;
Books are gates to lands of pleasure;
Books are paths that upward lead;
Books are friends. Come, let us read.

AUTHOR UNKNOWN

THERE IS NO FRIGATE LIKE A BOOK

There is no frigate like a book
    To take us lands away,
Nor any coursers like a page
    Of prancing poetry.

EMILY DICKINSON

WHO HATH A BOOK

Who hath a book
    Has friends at hand,
And gold and gear
    At his command;

And rich estates,
    If he but look,

187

Are held by him
Who hath a book.

Who hath a book
Has but to read
And he may be
A king indeed;

His kingdom is
His inglenook;
All this is his
Who hath a book.

WILBUR D. NESBIT

'TIS THE MIND THAT MAKES THE BODY RICH

'Tis the mind that makes the body rich;
And as the sun breaks through the darkest clouds,
So honor peereth in the meanest habit.

WILLIAM SHAKESPEARE, *THE TAMING OF THE SHREW* 4.3.173–75

Additional poems about knowledge and wisdom appear in the topics
"Character," "Example," "Truth," and elsewhere.

LIFE

GOD IS A FATHER

God is a Father.
Man is a brother.
Life is a mission
And not a career.

AUTHOR UNKNOWN

CONTENTED LIVING

Nine requisites for contented living:
Health enough to make work a pleasure;
Wealth enough to support your needs;
Strength to battle with difficulties and overcome them;
Grace enough to confess your sins and forsake them;
Patience enough to toil until some good is accomplished;
Charity enough to see some good in your neighbor;
Love enough to move you to be useful and helpful to others;
Faith enough to make real the things of God;
Hope enough to remove all anxious fears concerning the future.

JOHANN WOLFGANG VON GOETHE

MY CREED

To live as gently as I can;
To be, no matter where, a man;
To take what comes of good or ill,
And cling to faith and honor still;
To do my best, and let that stand
The record of my brain and hand;
And then, should failure come to me,
Still work and hope for victory.

To have no secret place wherein
I stoop unseen to shame or sin;
To be the same when I'm alone
As when my every deed is known;

To live undaunted, unafraid
Of any step that I have made;
To be without pretense or sham
Exactly what men think I am.

To leave some simple work behind
To keep my having lived in mind;
If enmity to aught I show,
To be an honest, generous foe;
To play my little part, nor whine
That greater honors are not mine.
This I believe is all I need
For my philosophy and creed.

EDGAR A. GUEST

WE LIVE IN DEEDS

We live in deeds, not years; in thought, not breath;
In feelings, not in figures on a dial.
We should count time by heart-throbs. He most lives
Who thinks most, feels the noblest, acts the best.
Life's but a means unto an end; that end
Beginning, mean, and end of all things—God.

PHILIP JAMES BAILEY

TALK HAPPINESS

Talk happiness. The world is sad enough
    Without your woe. No path is wholly rough;
Look for the places that are smooth and clear,
    And speak of those, to rest the weary ear
Of Earth, so hurt by one continuous strain
    Of human discontent and grief and pain.

Talk faith. The world is better off without
    Your uttered ignorance and morbid doubt.
If you have faith in God, or man, or self,
    Say so. If not, push back upon the shelf
Of silence, all your thoughts, till faith shall come;
    No one will grieve because your lips are dumb.

Talk health. The dreary, never-ending tale
　　Of mortal maladies is more than stale.
One cannot charm, or interest, or please
　　By harping on that minor chord, disease.
Say you are well, or all is well with you,
　　And God shall hear your words and make them true.

ELLA WHEELER WILCOX

FROM THE POWER OF LITTLES

Great events, we often find,
On little things depend,
And very small beginnings
Have oft a mighty end. . . .

Our life is made entirely
Of moments multiplied,
As little streamlets, joining,
Form the ocean's tide.

AUTHOR UNKNOWN

A PSALM OF LIFE
WHAT THE HEART OF THE YOUNG MAN SAID TO THE PSALMIST

Tell me not, in mournful numbers,
　　Life is but an empty dream!—
For the soul is dead that slumbers,
　　And things are not what they seem.

Life is real! Life is earnest!
　　And the grave is not its goal;
Dust thou art, to dust returnest,
　　Was not spoken of the soul.

Not enjoyment, and not sorrow,
　　Is our destined end or way;
But to act, that each to-morrow
　　Find us farther than to-day.

191

Art is long, and Time is fleeting,
  And our hearts, though stout and brave,
Still, like muffled drums, are beating
  Funeral marches to the grave.

In the world's broad field of battle,
  In the bivouac of Life,
Be not like dumb, driven cattle!
  Be a hero in the strife!

Trust no Future, howe'er pleasant!
  Let the dead Past bury its dead!
Act,—act in the living Present!
  Heart within, and God o'erhead!

Lives of great men all remind us
  We can make our lives sublime,
And, departing, leave behind us
  Footprints on the sands of time;

Footprints, that perhaps another,
  Sailing o'er life's solemn main,
A forlorn and shipwrecked brother,
  Seeing, shall take heart again.

Let us, then, be up and doing,
  With a heart for any fate;
Still achieving, still pursuing,
  Learn to labor and to wait.

HENRY WADSWORTH LONGFELLOW

ALL THE WORLD'S A STAGE

All the world's a stage,
And all the men and women merely players:
They have their exits and their entrances;
And one man in his time plays many parts.

WILLIAM SHAKESPEARE, *AS YOU LIKE IT* 2.7.139–42

LIFE'S BOOK

No matter what else you are doing,
    From cradle days through to the end,
You are writing your life's secret story,
    Each night sees another page penned.
Each month ends a thirty-page chapter;
    Each year, the end of a part;
And never an act is misstated,
    Nor even a wish of the heart.
Each morn when you wake, the book opens,
    Revealing a page clean and white;
What thoughts and what words and what doings
    Will cover its surface by night!
God leaves that to you—you the writer—
    And never one word will grow dim
Until someday you write the word "finish"
    And give back your life's book to Him.

AUTHOR UNKNOWN

LET ME BUT LIVE MY LIFE

Let me but live my life from year to year,
    With forward face and unreluctant soul.
    Not hurrying to, nor turning from the goal;
Not mourning for the things that disappear
In the dim past, nor holding back in fear
    From what the future veils; but with a whole
    And happy heart, that pays its toll
To youth and age, and travels on with cheer.
So let the way wind up the hill or down,
    O'er rough or smooth, the journey will be joy;
    Still seeking what I sought when but a boy,
New friendship, high adventure, and a crown,
    I shall grow old, but never lose life's zest,
    Because the road's last turn will be the best.

HENRY VAN DYKE

Additional poems about life appear in the topics "Adversity," "Success," "Work," and elsewhere.

LOVE

DESTINY

Somewhere there waiteth in this world of ours
   For one lone soul another lonely soul,
Each choosing each through all the weary hours.
   And meeting strangely at one sudden goal,
Then blend they, like green leaves with golden flowers,
   Into one beautiful perfect whole;
And life's long night is ended, and the way
   Lies open onward to eternal day.

SIR EDWIN ARNOLD

JENNY KISSED ME

Jenny kissed me when we met,
   Jumping from the chair she sat in.
Time, you thief! who love to get
   Sweets into your list, put that in.
Say I'm weary, say I'm sad;
   Say that health and wealth have missed me;
Say I'm growing old, but add—
   Jenny kissed me!

LEIGH HUNT

MY LIFE IS A BOWL

My life is a bowl which is mine to brim
   With loveliness old and new.
So I fill its clay from stem to rim
   With you, dear heart,
     With you.

My life is a pool which can only hold
   One star and a glimpse of blue.
But the blue and the little lamp of gold
   Are you, dear heart,
     Are you.

My life is a homing bird that flies
   Through the starry dusk and dew
Home to the heaven of your true eyes,
   Home, dear heart,
      To you.

MAY RILEY SMITH

LOVE'S PHILOSOPHY

The Fountains mingle with the River
   And the Rivers with the Ocean,
The winds of Heaven mix for ever
   With a sweet emotion;
Nothing in the world is single;
   All things by a law divine
In one spirit meet and mingle.
   Why not I with thine?

See the mountains kiss high Heaven
   And the waves clasp one another;
No sister-flower would be forgiven
   If it disdained its brother.
And the sunlight clasps the earth
   And the moonbeams kiss the sea:
What is all this sweet work worth
   If thou kiss not me?

PERCY BYSSHE SHELLEY

FAULTS

They came to tell your faults to me,
They named them over one by one;
I laughed aloud when they were done,
I knew them all so well before;—
Oh, they were blind, too blind to see
Your faults had made me love you more.

SARA TEASDALE

THE LARGER PRAYER

At first I prayed for Light:
  Could I but see the way,
How gladly, swiftly would I walk
  To everlasting day.

And next I prayed for Strength:
  That I might tread the road
With firm, unfaltering feet and win
  The heaven's serene abode.

And then I asked for Faith:
  Could I but trust my God,
I'd live enfolded in His peace,
  Though foes were all abroad.

But now I pray for Love:
  Deep love to God and man,
A living love that will not fail,
  However dark his plan.

And Light and Strength and Faith
Are opening everywhere;
God only waited for me, till
  I prayed the larger prayer.

EDNA DOW CHENEY

OH, HOW SKILLFUL GROWS THE HAND

Oh, how skillful grows the hand
That obeyeth love's command;
It is the heart, and not the brain
That to the highest doth attain,
And he who follows love's behest
Far exceedeth all the rest.

HENRY WADSWORTH LONGFELLOW

LOVE

I love you,
Not only for what you are,
But for what I am
When I am with you.

I love you,
Not only for what
You have made of yourself,
But for what
You are making of me.

I love you
For the part of me
That you bring out;
I love you
For putting your hand
Into my heaped-up heart
And passing over
All the foolish, weak things
That you can't help
Dimly seeing there,
And for drawing out
Into the light
All the beautiful belongings
That no one else has looked
Quite far enough to find.

I love you because you
Are helping me to make
Of the lumber of my life
Not a tavern
But a temple;
Out of the works
Of my every day
Not a reproach
But a song.

I love you
Because you have done
More than any creed

Could have done
To make me good,
And more than any fate
Could have done
To make me happy.

You have done it
Without a touch,
Without a word,
Without a sign.
You have done it
By being yourself.

Perhaps that is what
Being a friend means,
After all.

ROY CROFT

THE HOUSE OF PRIDE

I lived with Pride; the house was hung
    With tapestries of rich design.
Of many houses, this among
    Them all was richest, and 'twas mine.
But in the chambers burned no fire,
    Though all the furniture was gold:
I sickened of fulfilled desire,
    The House of Pride was very cold.

I lived with Knowledge; very high
    Her house rose on a mountain's side.
I watched the stars roll through the sky,
    I read the scroll of Time flung wide.
But in that house, austere and bare,
    No children played, no laughter clear
Was heard, no voice of mirth was there,
    The House was high but very drear.

I lived with Love; all she possessed
    Was but a tent beside a stream.
She warmed my cold hands in her breast,
    She wove around my sleep a dream.

And One there was with face divine
    Who softly came, when day was spent,
And turned our water into wine,
    And made our life a sacrament.

WILLIAM J. DAWSON

BELIEVE ME,
IF ALL THOSE ENDEARING YOUNG CHARMS

Believe me, if all those endearing young charms,
    Which I gaze on so fondly today,
Were to change by tomorrow, and fleet in my arms,
    Like fairy gifts fading away,
Thou wouldst still be adored, as this moment thou art,
    Let thy loveliness fade as it will,
And around the dear ruin each wish of my heart
    Would entwine itself verdantly still.

It is not while beauty and youth are thine own,
    And thy cheeks unprofaned by a tear,
That the fervor and faith of a soul can be known,
    To which time will but make thee more dear;
No, the heart that has truly loved never forgets,
    But as truly loves on to the close,
As the sunflower turns on her god, when he sets,
    The same look which she turned when he rose.

THOMAS MOORE

HIAWATHA'S WOOING
FROM *THE SONG OF HIAWATHA*

As unto the bow the cord is,
So unto the man is woman,
Though she bends him, she obeys him,
Though she draws him, yet she follows,
Useless each without the other!

HENRY WADSWORTH LONGFELLOW

TO MY DEAR AND LOVING HUSBAND

If ever two were one, then surely we.
If ever man were loved by wife, then thee;

If ever wife was happy in a man,
Compare with me ye women if you can.
I prize thy love more than whole mines of gold,
Or all the riches that the East doth hold.
My love is such that rivers cannot quench,
Nor ought but love from thee give recompense.
Thy love is such I can no way repay;
The heavens reward thee manifold, I pray.
Then while we live, in love let's so persever,
That when we live no more we may live ever.

ANNE BRADSTREET

SONNET 116

Let me not to the marriage of true minds
Admit impediments. Love is not love
Which alters when it alteration finds,
Or bends with the remover to remove:
O, no! it is an ever-fixèd mark,
That looks on tempests and is never shaken;
It is the star to every wandering bark,
Whose worth's unknown, although his height be taken.
Love's not Time's fool, though rosy lips and cheeks
Within his bending sickle's compass come;
Love alters not with his brief hours and weeks,
But bears it out even to the edge of doom.
　　If this be error, and upon me proved,
　　I never writ, nor no man ever loved.

WILLIAM SHAKESPEARE

SONNET 43
FROM *SONNETS FROM THE PORTUGUESE*

How do I love thee? Let me count the ways.
I love thee to the depth and breadth and height
My soul can reach, when feeling out of sight
For the ends of Being and ideal Grace.
I love thee to the level of everyday's
Most quiet need, by sun and candle-light.
I love thee freely, as men strive for Right;
I love thee purely, as they turn from Praise.

I love thee with the passion put to use
In my old griefs, and with my childhood's faith.
I love thee with a love I seemed to lose
With my lost saints—I love thee with the breath,
Smiles, tears, of all my life!—and, if God choose,
I shall but love thee better after death.

ELIZABETH BARRETT BROWNING

LOVE LIVES BEYOND THE TOMB

Love lives beyond
The tomb, the earth, which fades like dew—
I love the fond,
The faithful, and the true.

Love lies in sleep,
'Tis happiness of healthy dreams,
Eve's dews may weep,
But love delightful seems.

'Tis seen in flowers,
And in the even's pearly dew,
On earth's green hours,
And in the heaven's eternal blue.

'Tis heard in Spring
When light and sunbeams, warm and kind,
On angel's wing
Bring love and music to the mind.

And where's the voice,
So young, so beautiful, and sweet
As Nature's choice,
Where Spring and lovers meet?

Love lives beyond
The tomb, the earth, the flowers, and dew.
I love the fond,
The faithful, young, and true.

JOHN CLARKE

I WED THEE FOREVER

I wed thee forever, not for now,
Not for the sham of earth's brief years,
I wed thee for the life beyond the tears,
Beyond the heart pain and clouded brow.
Love knows no grave and it shall guide us dear
When life's spent candles flutter and burn low.

ANDERSON MONROE BATEN

ALL PATHS LEAD TO YOU

All paths lead to you
    Where e'er I stray,
You are the evening star
    At the end of day.

All paths lead to you
    Hill-top or low,
You are the white birch
    In the sun's glow.

All paths lead to you
    Where e'er I roam.
You are the lark-song
    Calling me home!

BLANCHE SHOEMAKER WAGSTAFF

Additional poems about love appear in the topics "Friendship," "Home and Family," and elsewhere.

MEMORIAL DAY

IN FLANDERS FIELDS

In Flanders fields the poppies blow
Between the crosses, row on row,
    That mark our place; and in the sky
    The larks, still bravely singing, fly,
Scarce heard amid the guns below.

We are the Dead. Short days ago
We lived, felt dawn, saw sunset glow,
    Loved and were loved, and now we lie
    In Flanders fields.

Take up our quarrel with the foe:
To you from falling hands we throw
    The torch; be yours to hold it high!
    If ye break faith with us who die
We shall not sleep, though poppies grow
    In Flanders fields.

JOHN McCRAE

MEMORIAL DAY

These did not pass in selfishness; they died for all mankind;
They died to build a better world for all who stay behind;
And we who hold their memory dear, and bring them flowers to-day,
Should consecrate ourselves once more to live and die as they.

These were defenders of the faith and guardians of the truth;
That you and I might live and love, they gladly gave their youth;
And we who set this day apart to honor them who sleep
Should pledge ourselves to hold the faith they gave their lives to keep.

If tears are all we shed for them, then they have died in vain;
If flowers are all we bring them now, forgotten they remain;
If by their courage we ourselves to courage are not led,
Then needlessly these graves have closed above our heroes dead.

EDGAR A. GUEST

MEMORIAL DAY
"DULCE ET DECORUM EST"

The bugle echoes shrill and sweet,
    But not of war it sings to-day.
The road is rhythmic with the feet
    Of men-at-arms who come to pray.

The roses blossom white and red
    On tombs where weary soldiers lie;
Flags wave above the honored dead
    And martial music cleaves the sky.

Above their wreath-strewn graves we kneel,
    They kept the faith and fought the fight.
Through flying lead and crimson steel
    They plunged for Freedom and the Right.

May we, their grateful children, learn
    Their strength, who lie beneath this sod,
Who went through fire and death to earn
    At last the accolade of God.

In shining rank on rank arrayed
    They march, the legions of the Lord;
He is their Captain unfraid,
    The Prince of Peace . . . Who brought a sword.

JOYCE KILMER

AWAY

I cannot say, and I will not say
That he is dead. He is just away!
With a cheery smile, and a wave of the hand,
He has wandered into an unknown land,
And left us dreaming how very fair
It needs must be, since he lingers there.
And you—O you, who the wildest yearn
For the old-time step and the glad return,
Think of him faring on, as dear
In the love of There as the love of Here;
And loyal still, as he gave the blows

Of his warrior-strength to his country's foes.
Mild and gentle, as he was brave,
When the sweetest love of his life he gave
To simple things: Where the violets grew
Blue as the eyes they were liken to,
The touches of his hands have strayed
As reverently as his lips have prayed:
When the little brown thrush that harshly chirred
Was dear to him as the mocking-bird;
And he pitied as much as a man in pain
A writhing honey-bee wet with rain.
Think of him still as the same, I say:
He is not dead—he is just away!

JAMES WHITCOMB RILEY

EVER NEAR US

Ever near us though unseen,
    The dear immortal spirits tread,
And all the universe is life;
    There is no dead.

AUTHOR UNKNOWN

Additional poems that are appropriate for Memorial Day appear in the topics "Death and Immortality," "Jesus Christ," and elsewhere.

MILLENNIAL AGE

THE SPRING OF GOD
FROM "IN APRIL ONCE"

Across the edges of the world there blows a wind
Mysterious with perfume of a Spring;
A Spring that is not of the kindling earth,
That's more than scent of bloom or gleam of bud;
The Spring of God in flower!
Down there where neither sun nor air came through,
I felt it blow across my dungeon walls—

The wind before the footsteps of the Lord!
It bloweth now across the world;
It strangely stirs the hearts of men; wars cease;
Rare deeds familiar grow; fastings and prayers,
Forgiveness, poverty; temples are built
On visioned impulses, and children march
On journeys with no end.
Far off, far off He comes,
And we are swept upon our knees
As meadow grasses kneeling to the wind.

WILLIAM A. PERCY

PARADISE

Once in a dream I saw the flowers
   That bud and bloom in Paradise;
   More fair are they than waking eyes
Have seen in all this world of ours.
And faint the perfume-bearing rose,
   And faint the lily on its stem,
And faint the perfect violet,
   Compared with them.

I heard the songs of paradise;
   Each bird sat singing in its place;
   A tender song so full of grace
It soared like incense to the skies.

206

Each bird sat singing to its mate
   Soft cooing notes among the trees:
The nightingale herself were cold
   To such as these.

I saw the fourfold River flow,
   And deep it was, with golden sand;
   It flowed between a mossy land
With murmured music grave and low.
It hath refreshment for all thirst,
   For fainting spirits strength and rest:
Earth holds not such a draught as this
   From east to west.

The Tree of Life stood budding there,
   Abundant with its twelvefold fruits;
   Eternal sap sustains its roots,
Its shadowing branches fill the air.
Its leaves are healing for the world,
   Its fruit the hungry world can feed
Sweeter than honey to the taste
   And balm indeed.

I saw the Gate called Beautiful;
   And looked, but scarce could look within;
I saw the golden streets begin,
And outskirts of the glassy pool.
Oh harps, oh crowns of plenteous stars,
   Oh green palm-branches, many-leaved—
Eye hath not seen, nor ear hath heard,
   Nor heart conceived.

I hope to see these things again,
   But not as once in dreams by night;
   To see them with my very sight,
And touch and handle and attain:
To have all heaven beneath my feet
   For narrow way that once they trod;
   To have my part with all the saints
   And with my God.

CHRISTINA ROSSETTI

THE NEW AGE

When navies are forgotten
   And fleets are useless things,
When the dove shall warm her bosom
   Beneath the eagle's wings;

When the memory of battles
   At last is strange and old,
When nations have one banner
   And creeds have found one fold;

When the Hand that sprinkles midnight
   With its dust of powdered suns
Has hushed this tiny tumult
   Of sects, and swords, and guns,

Then hate's last note of discord
   In all God's world shall cease
In the conquest which is service,
   In the victory which is peace!

FREDERICK LAWRENCE KNOWLES

HAIL TO THE BRIGHTNESS
OF ZION'S GLAD MORNING!

Hail to the brightness of Zion's glad morning!
Joy to the lands that in darkness have lain!
Hushed be the accents of sorrow and mourning.
Zion in triumph begins her glad reign.

Hail to the brightness of Zion's glad morning,
Long by the prophets of Israel foretold!
Hail to the millions from bondage returning!
Gentiles and Jews the glad vision behold.

Lo! in the desert the flowers are springing;
Streams, ever copious, are gliding along.
Loud from the mountaintops echoes are ringing;
Wastes rise in verdure and mingle in song.

Hark! from all lands, from the isles of the ocean,
Praise to Jehovah ascending on high.
Fallen the engines of war and commotion;
Shouts of salvation are rending the sky.

THOMAS HASTINGS

LOOKING FORWARD

I dream of a glorious future,
Of a bright and better day
When every living creature
God's mandates will obey;

When no one will go hungry
Nor plead for daily bread;
No hearts be overburdened
With anguish, fear, and dread.

When every man will find a friend
In every other man,
And each will seek the good of all
According to God's plan;

When enmity shall disappear,
And wars be waged no more,
But peace and love and beauty
Abound from shore to shore;

When no weapons of destruction,
Designed by human hands,
Shall terrify the nations
Or devastate their lands;

When no homeless, starving children
Shall wander here and there,
'Mid scenes of desolation
And moans of wild despair.

O Father, send repentance
That we may sense our shame
And realize with penitence
We have ourselves to blame.

Hasten, Lord, the promised day,
When wickedness shall end
And Christ shall reign in glory,
Our Brother and our Friend.

Then will the hills and valleys sing,
All peoples bend the knee
And listen to the words of God
On glories yet to be!

RUTH MAY FOX

COME, LET US ANEW

Come, let us anew our journey pursue,
Roll round with the year,
And never stand still till the Master appear.
His adorable will let us gladly fulfill,
And our talents improve
By the patience of hope and the labor of love.

Our life as a dream, our time as a stream
Glide swiftly away,
And the fugitive moment refuses to stay;
For the arrow is flown and the moments are gone.
The millennial year
Presses on to our view, and eternity's here.

Oh, that each in the day of His coming may say,
"I have fought my way thru;
I have finished the work thou didst give me to do."
Oh, that each from his Lord may receive the glad word:
"Well and faithfully done;
Enter into my joy and sit down on my throne."

CHARLES WESLEY

THY KINGDOM COME

Thy kingdom come—on bended knee
    The passing ages pray;
And faithful souls have yearned to see
    On earth that kingdom's day.

210

But the slow watches of the night
   Not less to God belong,
And for the everlasting right
   The silent stars are strong.

And lo! already on the hills
   The flags of dawn appear;
Gird up your loins, ye prophet souls,
   Proclaim the day is near:

The day in whose clear shining light
   All wrong shall stand revealed,
When justice shall be clothed with might,
   And every hurt be healed:

When knowledge, hand in hand with peace,
   Shall walk the earth abroad,—
The day of perfect righteousness,
   The promised day of God.

Frederick L. Hosmer

FROM ALL THAT DWELL BELOW THE SKIES

From all that dwell below the skies,
Let the Creator's praise arise;
Let the Redeemer's name be sung
Through ev'ry land, by ev'ry tongue.

In ev'ry land begin the song;
To ev'ry land the strains belong.
In cheerful sounds all voices raise
And fill the world with loudest praise.

Your lofty themes, ye mortals, bring;
In songs of praise divinely sing.
The great salvation loud proclaim,
And shout for joy the Savior's name.

Eternal are thy mercies, Lord;
Eternal truth attends thy word.
Thy praise shall sound from shore to shore,
Till suns shall rise and set no more.

Isaac Watts

THE CITY OF OUR HOPES

Hail the glorious Golden City,
    Pictured by the seers of old!
Everlasting light shines o'er it,
    Wondrous tales of it are told:
Only righteous men and women
    Dwell within its gleaming wall;
Wrong is banished from its borders,
    Justice reigns supreme o'er all.

We are builders of that city;
    All our joys and all our groans
Help to rear its shining ramparts;
    All our lives are building stones
Whether humble or exalted,
    All are called to task divine;
All must aid alike to carry
    Forward one sublime design.

And the work that we have builded,
    Oft with bleeding hands and tears,
Oft in error, oft in anguish,
    Will not perish with our years:
It will live and shine transfigured
    In the final reign of Right;
It will merge into the splendors
    Of the City of the Light.

FELIX ADLER

Additional poems about the Millennial Age appear in the topic "Jesus Christ" and elsewhere.

MOTHERHOOD

MOTHER'S LOVE

Her love is like an island
    In life's ocean, vast and wide,
A peaceful, quiet shelter
    From the wind, and rain, and tide.

'Tis bound on the north by Hope,
    By Patience on the west,
By tender Counsel on the south,
    And on the east by Rest.

Above it like a beacon light
    Shine Faith, and Truth, and Prayer;
And through the changing scenes of life,
    I find a haven there.

AUTHOR UNKNOWN

WHICH LOVED BEST?

"I love you, Mother," said little John;
Then, forgetting his work, his cap went on,
And he was off to the garden swing,
And left her the water and wood to bring.

"I love you, Mother," said rosy Nell—
"I love you better than tongue can tell";
Then she teased and pouted full half the day,
Till her mother rejoiced when she went to play.

"I love you, Mother," said little Fan;
"Today I'll help you all I can;
How glad I am that school doesn't keep!"
So she rocked the babe till it fell asleep.

Then, stepping softly, she fetched the broom,
And swept the floor and tidied the room;
Busy and happy all day was she,
Helpful and happy as child could be.

"I love you, Mother," again they said,
Three little children going to bed;
How do you think that Mother guessed
Which of them really loved her best?

JOY ALLISON

MOTHER

Sometimes when I get home from school
And mother isn't there,
And though I know she'll be back soon
And I don't really care,
Still all the furniture looks queer,
The house seems hushed and sad:
And then I hear her coming in,
And, oh boy, am I glad!

ESTHER HULL DOOLITTLE

I FEEL

I feel that, in the Heavens above,
The angels, whispering to one another,
Can find, among their burning terms of love,
None so devotional as that of *Mother.*

EDGAR ALLAN POE

THE NAME OF MOTHER

The holiest words my tongue can frame,
The noblest thoughts my soul can claim,
Unworthy are to praise the name
More precious than all other.
An infant, when her love first came,
A man, I find it still the same,
Reverently I breathe her name,
The blessed name of mother.

GEORGE GRIFFITH FETHER

THE HAND THAT ROCKS THE CRADLE
IS THE HAND THAT RULES THE WORLD

They say that man is mighty,
   He governs land and sea;
He wields a mighty scepter
   O'er lesser powers that be;
But a mightier power and stronger
   Man from his throne has hurled;
For the hand that rocks the cradle
   Is the hand that rules the world.

Blessing on the hand of women!
   Angels guard its strength and grace,
In the palace, cottage, hovel,
   Oh, no matter where the place;
Would that never storms assailed it,
   Rainbows ever gently curled;
For the hand that rocks the cradle
   Is the hand that rules the world. . . .

Woman, how divine your mission
   Here upon our natal sod!
Keep, oh, keep the young heart open
   Always to the breath of God!
All true trophies of the ages
   Are from mother-love impearled;
For the hand that rocks the cradle
   Is the hand that rules the world.

WILLIAM ROSS WALLACE

MY MOTHER

Who fed me from her gentle breast
And hushed me in her arms to rest,
And on my cheek sweet kisses pressed?
   My mother.

When sleep forsook my open eye,
Who was it sung sweet lullaby
And rocked me that I should not cry?
   My mother.

Who sat and watched my infant head
When sleeping in my cradle bed,
And tears of sweet affection shed?
  My mother.

When pain and sickness made me cry,
Who gazed upon my heavy eye
And wept, for fear that I should die?
  My mother.

Who ran to help me when I fell
And would some pretty story tell,
Or kiss the part to make it well?
  My mother.

Who taught my infant lips to pray,
To love God's holy word and day,
And walk in wisdom's pleasant way?
  My mother.

And can I ever cease to be
Affectionate and kind to thee
Who wast so very kind to me,—
  My mother.

Oh no, the thought I cannot bear;
And if God please my life to spare
I hope I shall reward thy care,
  My mother.

When thou art feeble, old and gray,
My healthy arm shall be thy stay,
And I will soothe thy pains away,
  My mother.

And when I see thee hang thy head,
'Twill be my turn to watch thy bed,
And tears of sweet affection shed,—
  My mother.

JANE TAYLOR

MOTHERS

Mothers are people who cook things
Like breakfast or lunch or a snack;
Dexterous people who hook things
Which button or zip up the back.
Mothers are people who blow things,
Balloons and kisses and noses;
Green-thumbish people who grow things
Like ivy and puppies and roses.
Mothers are people who send things
Like letters and strawberry tarts;
Magical people who mend things
Like blue jeans and elbows and hearts.
Mothers are people who find things
Like mittens and homework and germs;
Fussbudget people who mind things
Like cusswords and snowballs and worms.
Mothers are people who sweep things
Like porches and cobwebs and rugs.
Softhearted people who keep things
Like artwork, report cards, and hugs.
Mothers are people who nurse things,
A boy or a girl or a spouse.
And all in all there are worse things
Than mothers to have in your house.

AUTHOR UNKNOWN

TRIBUTE TO A MOTHER

Faith that withstood the shocks of toil and time;
    Hope that defied despair;
    Patience that conquered care;
And loyalty, whose courage was sublime;
The great deep heart that was a home for all—
    Just, eloquent, and strong
    In protest against wrong;
Wide charity, that knew no sin, no fall;
The Spartan spirit that made life so grand,
    Mating poor daily needs

With high, heroic deeds,
That wrested happiness from Fate's hard hand.

LOUISA MAY ALCOTT

FAITH

"Keep this for me."
What child has not said this,
And placed a treasure in his Mother's hand
With strict injunction she should keep it safe
Till he return?
He knows with her it will be safe;
No troubled thought or anxious fear besets his mind,
And off he runs light-hearted to his play.

If children can so trust, why cannot we,
And place our treasures, too, in God's safe hand;
Our hopes, ambitions, needs, and those we love,
Just see them, in his all embracing care,
And say with joyous heart, "They are with Thee."

AUTHOR UNKNOWN

MOTHER'S DAY

Let every day be Mother's Day!
Make roses grow along her way
    And beauty everywhere.
Oh, never let her eyes be wet
With tears of sorrow or regret,
    And never cease to care!
Come, grown up children, and rejoice
That you can hear your mother's voice!

A day for her! For you she gave
Long years of love and service brave;
    For you her youth was spent.
There was no weight of hurt to care
Too heavy for her strength to bear;
    She followed where you went;
Her courage and her love sublime
You could depend on all the time.

218

No day or night she set apart
On which to open wide her heart
   And welcome you within;
There was no hour you would not be
First in her thought and memory,
   Though you were black with sin!
Though skies were gray or skies were blue
Not once has she forgotten you.

Let every day be Mother's Day!
With love and roses strew her way,
   And smiles of joy and pride!
Come, grown up children, to the knee
Where long ago you used to be
   And never turn aside;
Oh, never let her eyes grow wet
With tears, because her babes forget.

Edgar A. Guest

THE BRAVEST BATTLE

The bravest battle that ever was fought,
   Shall I tell you where and when,
On the maps of the world you will find it not;
   It was fought by the mothers of men.

Nay, not with cannon or battle shot,
   With sword or braver pen;
Nay, not with eloquent word or thought,
   From the mouths of wonderful men.

But deep in a woman's walled-up heart—
   Of woman that would not yield,
But patiently, silently bore her part—
   Lo! there in that battlefield.

No marshaling troop, no bivouac song;
   No banners to gleam and wave;
And oh! these battles they last so long—
   From babyhood to the grave!

Yet, faithful still as a bridge of stars,
    She fights in her walled-up town—
Fights on and on in the endless wars,
    Then silent, unseen—goes down.

JOAQUIN MILLER

MOTHERHOOD IS . . .

The purest joy the heart can feel,
The strongest bond that love can seal,
The deepest truth that life can teach,
The greatest height the soul can reach.

FLORA S. HORNE

TWO TEMPLES

A builder builded a temple,
He wrought it with grace and skill;
Pillars and groins and arches
All fashioned to work his will.
Men said, as they saw its beauty,
"It shall never know decay;
Great is thy skill, O builder!
Thy fame shall endure for aye."

A mother builded a temple
With loving and infinite care,
Planning each arch with patience,
Laying each stone with prayer.
None praised her unceasing efforts,
None knew of her wondrous plan,
For the temple the mother builded
Was unseen by the eyes of man.

Gone is the builder's temple,
Crumpled into the dust;
Low lies each stately pillar,
Food for consuming rust.
But the temple the mother builded
Will last while the ages roll,

For that beautiful unseen temple
Was a child's immortal soul.

HATTIE VOSE HALL

TRUE COURAGE

The wife who girds her husband's sword,
   'Mid little ones who weep or wonder,
And bravely speaks the cheering word,
   What though her heart be rent asunder,
Doomed nightly in her dreams to hear
   The bolts of death around him rattle,
Has shed as sacred blood as e'er
   Was poured upon a field of battle.

The mother who conceals her grief,
   While to her breast her son she presses,
Then breathes a few brave words and brief,
   Kissing the patriot brow she blesses;
With no one but her secret God to know
   The pain that weighs upon her;
Sheds holy blood as e'er the sod
   Received on freedom's field of honor.

AUTHOR UNKNOWN

WATCHING FOR US

She always leaned to watch for us,
   Anxious if we were late,
In winter by the window,
   In summer by the gate;

And though we mocked her tenderly,
   Who had such foolish care,
The long way home would seem more safe
   Because she waited there.

Her thoughts were all so full of us—
   She never could forget!
And so I think that where she is
   She must be watching yet.

Waiting till we come home to her,
  Anxious if we are late—
Watching from heaven's window,
  Leaning from heaven's gate.

MARGARET WIDDEMER

BACKWARD

Backward, turn backward, O Time, in your flight,
  Make me a child again just for tonight!
Mother, come back from the echoless shore,
  Take me again to your heart, as of yore;
Kiss from my forehead the furrows of care,
  Smooth the few silver threads out of my hair;
Over my slumbers your loving watch keep,
  Rock me to sleep, Mother, rock me to sleep.

ELIZABETH AKERS ALLEN

*Additional poems about motherhood appear in the topics "Home and Family,"
"Love," and elsewhere.*

NATURE

THIS IS MY FATHER'S WORLD

This is my Father's world,
And to my listening ears
All nature sings, and round me rings
The music of the spheres.
This is my Father's world:
I rest me in the thought
Of rocks and trees, of skies and seas;
His hand the wonders wrought.

This is my Father's world,
The birds their carols raise,
The morning light, the lily white,
Declare their Maker's praise.
This is my Father's world:
He shines in all that's fair;
In the rustling grass I hear Him pass,
He speaks to me everywhere.

MALTBIE D. BABCOCK

FROM THE VISION OF SIR LAUNFAL

Every clod feels a stir of might,
An instinct within it that reaches and towers,
And groping blindly above it for light,
Climbs to a soul in grass and flowers.

JAMES RUSSELL LOWELL

AT COOL OF DAY

At cool of day, with God I walk
My garden's grateful shade;
I hear his voice among the trees
And I am not afraid.

CAROLINE ATHERTON MASON

GOD'S BOOK

God spreads a book before my eyes,
    As I go tramping hill and dell,
And oh, my heart is made most wise
    By what His wind-blown pages tell.

Though men declare I am a clown,
    Whose dreams have made him worse than fey,
The while I wander up and down,
    I give no heed to what they say.

I turn me from their foolish words
    To read the kindliness of God
Within His book of singing birds,
    Of trees and brooks and fragrant sod.

EDGAR DANIEL KRAMER

MY HEART LEAPS UP

My heart leaps up when I behold
    A rainbow in the sky:
So was it when my life began;
So is it now I am a man;
So be it when I shall grow old,
    Or let me die!
The Child is father of the Man;
And I could wish my days to be
Bound each to each by natural piety.

WILLIAM WORDSWORTH

THE SILENT PLACES

I have come back from the mountains,
    And the beauty of forest ways,
From the pine-trail winding at sunset
    To the crags in the purple haze.

I have come back from the prairies,
    And the free-born winds of the west,
Where my soul reached out to heaven,
    And found in the starlight rest.

I have come back to the city,
　　With its clang and its screech and its din;
Its halls are filled with madness,
　　And its eyes are blind with sin.

I think of the peaks white-crested,
　　And the sage on the sweeping plain,
And the vastness, and the silence,
　　And the whisper of God again.

I will go back to my mountains,
　　Back to the prairies I've trod;
Some day I shall stand in that silence
　　And speak once more with my God.

HAROLD M. HILDRETH

FLOWER IN THE CRANNIED WALL

Flower in the crannied wall,
I pluck you out of the crannies,
I hold you here, root and all, in my hand,
Little flower—but *if* I could understand
What you are, root and all, and all in all,
I should know what God and man is.

ALFRED, LORD TENNYSON

EARTH'S COMMON THINGS

Seek not afar for beauty. Lo! it glows
　　In dew-wet grasses all about thy feet;
　　In birds, in sunshine, childish faces sweet,
In stars and mountain summits topped with snows.

Go not abroad for happiness. For see,
　　It is a flower that blossoms at thy door!
　　Bring love and justice home, and then no more
Thou'lt wonder in what dwelling joy may be.

Dream not of noble service elsewhere wrought;
　　The simple duty that awaits thy hand
　　Is God's voice uttering a divine command,
Life's common deeds build all that saints have thought.

In wonder-workings, or some bush aflame,
   Men look for God and fancy Him concealed;
   But in earth's common things He stands revealed
While grass and flowers and stars spell out His name.

MINOT J. SAVAGE

FROM AUGURIES OF INNOCENCE

To see a World in a Grain of Sand
And a Heaven in a Wild Flower,
Hold Infinity in the palm of your hand
And Eternity in an hour.

WILLIAM BLAKE

THE YEAR'S AT THE SPRING

The year's at the spring
And day's at the morn;
Morning's at seven:
The hillside's dew-pearled;
The lark's on the wing;
The snail's on the thorn;
God's in his heaven—
All's right with the world!

ROBERT BROWNING

NATURE'S CREED

I believe in the brook as it wanders
   From hillside into glade;
I believe in the breeze as it whispers
   When evening's shadows fade.
I believe in the roar of the river
   As it dashes from high cascade;
I believe in the cry of the tempest
   'Mid the thunder's cannonade.
I believe in the light of shining stars,
   I believe in the sun and the moon;
I believe in the flash of lightning,
   I believe in the night-bird's croon.

I believe in the faith of the flowers,
I believe in the rock and sod,
For in all of these appeareth clear
The handiwork of God.

AUTHOR UNKNOWN

EARTH'S CRAMMED WITH HEAVEN

Earth's crammed with Heaven
And every common bush afire with God.
But only he who sees takes off his shoes.

ELIZABETH BARRETT BROWNING

RAIN

Rain was made for our delight.
A million little dancing feet
Down a patent-leather street
On a dusty summer night.

Sprites of silver at their play,
Down the canyon walls they chase,
Gay and gentle, to erase
The tired faces of the day.

To close in sleep the city's eyes,
Singing at a window pane
A murmuring and soft refrain
Of earth's own ancient lullabies.

BIANCA BRADBURY

I FIND EARTH NOT GRAY

I find earth not gray, but rosey,
Heaven not grim, but fair of hue.
Do I stoop? I pluck a posey;
Do I stand and stare? All's blue.

ROBERT BROWNING

THE LORD GOD PLANTED A GARDEN

The Lord God planted a garden
   In the first white days of the world,
And he set there an angel warden
   In a garment of light enfurled.

So near to the peace of Heaven,
   That the hawk might nest with the wren,
For there in the cool of the even'
   God walked with the first of men.

The kiss of the sun for pardon,
   The song of the birds for mirth—
One is nearer God's heart in a garden
   Than anywhere else on earth.

DOROTHY FRANCES GURNEY

TREES

I think that I shall never see
A poem lovely as a tree.
A tree whose hungry mouth is pressed
Against the earth's sweet flowing breast;
A tree that looks at God all day,
And lifts her leafy arms to pray;
A tree that may in Summer wear
A nest of robins in her hair;
Upon whose bosom snow has lain;
Who intimately lives with rain.
Poems are made by fools like me,
But only God can make a tree.

JOYCE KILMER

Additional poems about nature appear in the topics "God," "Happiness," "Life," and elsewhere.

228

NEW YEAR

THE NEW LEAF

He came to my desk with quivering lip—
    The lesson was done.
"Dear Teacher, I want a new leaf," he said,
    "I have spoiled this one."
I took the old leaf, stained and blotted,
And gave him a new one, all unspotted,
    And into his sad eyes smiled:
    "Do better now, my child!"

I went to the Throne with a quivering soul—
    The old year was done.
"Dear Father, hast Thou a new leaf for me?
    I have spoiled this one."
He took the old leaf, stained and blotted,
And gave me a new one, all unspotted,
    And into my sad heart smiled:
    "Do better now, my child!"

HELEN FIELD FISHER

THE MESSAGE OF THE NEW YEAR

I asked the New Year for some message sweet,
Some rule of life with which to guide my feet;
I asked, and paused: he answered soft and low,
    "God's will to know."

"Will knowledge then suffice, New Year?" I cried;
And, ere the question into silence died,
The answer came, "Nay, but remember, too,
    God's will to do."

Once more I asked, "Is there no more to tell?"
And once again the answer sweetly fell,
"Yes! this thing, all other things above:
    God's will to love."

AUTHOR UNKNOWN

RING OUT, WILD BELLS
FROM *IN MEMORIAM*

Ring out, wild bells, to the wild sky,
    The flying cloud, the frosty light:
    The year is dying in the night;
Ring out, wild bells, and let him die.

Ring out the old; ring in the new,
    Ring, happy bells, across the snow:
    The year is going, let him go;
Ring out the false, ring in the true.

Ring out the grief that saps the mind,
    For those that here we see no more;
    Ring out the feud of rich and poor,
Ring in redress to all mankind.

Ring out a slowly dying cause,
    And ancient forms of party strife;
    Ring in the nobler modes of life,
With sweeter manners, purer laws.

Ring out the want, the care, the sin,
    The faithless coldness of the times;
    Ring out, ring out my mournful rhymes,
But ring the fuller minstrel in.

Ring out false pride in place and blood,
    The civic slander and the spite;
    Ring in the love of truth and right,
Ring in the common love of good.

Ring out old shapes of foul disease;
    Ring out the narrowing lust of gold;
    Ring out the thousand wars of old,
Ring in the thousand years of peace.

Ring in the valiant men and free,
    The larger heart, the kindlier hand;
    Ring out the darkness of the land,
Ring in the Christ that is to be.

ALFRED, LORD TENNYSON

THE NEW YEAR

A flower unblown; a book unread;
A tree with fruit unharvested;
A path untrod; a house whose rooms
Lack yet the heart's divine perfumes:
A landscape whose wide border lies
In silent shade, 'neath silent skies;
A treasure with its gifts concealed—
This is the year that for you waits
Beyond tomorrow's mystic gates.

HORATIO NELSON POWERS

OLD YEARS AND NEW

Old years and new years, all blended into one,
The best of what there is to be, the best of what is gone—
Let's bury all the failures in the dim and dusty past
And keep the smiles of friendship and laughter to the last.

Old years and new years, life's in the making still;
We haven't come to glory yet, but there's the hope we will;
The dead old year was twelve months long, but now from it we're
    free,
And what's one year of good or bad to all the years to be?

Old years and new years, we need them one and all
To reach the dome of character and build its sheltering wall;
Past failures tried the souls of us, but if their tests we stood,
The sum of what we are to be may yet be counted good.

EDGAR A. GUEST

NEW YEAR

How burn the stars unchanging in the midnight skies,
    As on the earth the old year dies!
Like leaves before the storm, so haste our lives away;
    Eternal God, to Thee we pray.

For all Thy mercies past we lift our hearts in praise,
    Thy care that crowned our fleeting days;

231

Our follies and our sins, O Lord, remember not,
    Lost hours when we Thy love forgot.

From age to age Thy love endures; Thou art our God.
    Send now Thy flaming truth abroad,
That with the New Year's dawning right may conquer wrong,
    Grief yield to joy, and tears to song!

JOHN J. MOMENT

A LITTLE PRAYER

That I may not in blindness grope,
    But that I may with vision clear
Know when to speak a word of hope
    Or add a little wholesome cheer.

That tempered winds may softly blow
    Where little children, thinly clad,
Sit dreaming, when the flame is low,
    Of comforts they have never had.

That through the year which lies ahead
    No heart shall ache, no cheek be wet,
For any word that I have said
    Or profit I have tried to get.

S. E. KISER

JANUARY

We pause beside this door:
Thy year, O God, how shall we enter in?
The footsteps of a Child
Sound close beside us. Listen, he will speak!
His birthday bells have hardly rung a week,
Yet has he trod the worlds press undefiled.
Enter through me, he saith, nor wander more;
For lo! I am the Door.

LUCY LARCOM

Additional poems that are appropriate for the New Year appear in the topics "Hope," "Opportunity," and elsewhere.

OPPORTUNITY

USE WELL THE MOMENT

Use well the moment; what the hour
Brings for thy use is in thy power;
And what thou best canst understand
Is just the thing lies nearest to thy hand.

JOHANN WOLFGANG VON GOETHE

OPPORTUNITY

They do me wrong who say I come no more
    When once I knock and fail to find you in;
For every day I stand outside your door
    And bid you wake, and rise to fight and win.

Wail not for precious chances passed away!
Weep not for golden ages on the wane!
Each night I burn the records of the day—
    At sunrise every soul is born again!

Dost thou behold thy lost youth all aghast?
    Dost reel from righteous retribution's blow?
Then turn from blotted archives of the past
    And find the future's pages white as snow.

Art thou a mourner? Rouse thee from thy spell;
    Art thou a sinner? Sins may be forgiven;
Each morning gives thee wings to fly from hell,
    Each night a star to guide thy feet to heaven.

Laugh like a boy at splendors that have sped,
    To vanished joys be blind and deaf and dumb;
My judgments seal the dead past with the dead,
    But never bind a moment yet to come.

Though deep in mire, wring not your hands and weep;
    I lend my arm to all who say, "I can!"

No shame-faced outcast ever sank so deep,
But yet might rise again and be a man!

WALTER MALONE

FROM MAUD MULLER

For of all sad words of tongue or pen,
The saddest are these: "It might have been!"

JOHN GREENLEAF WHITTIER

THERE IS A TIDE

There is a tide in the affairs of men
Which taken at the flood leads on to fortune;
Omitted, all the voyage of their life
Is bound in shallows and in miseries.
On such a full sea are we now afloat,
And we must take the current when it serves,
Or lose our ventures.

WILLIAM SHAKESPEARE, JULIUS CAESAR 4.3.218–23

SALUTATION OF THE DAWN

Look to this day,
For it is life, the very life of life!
In its brief course be all the verities
And realities of your existence.

The glory of action,
The bliss of growth,
The splendor of beauty.

For yesterday is but a dream
And tomorrow is only a vision;
But today, well-lived, makes
Every yesterday a dream of happiness
And every tomorrow a vision of hope.

Look well, therefore, to this day.
Such is the salutation of the dawn.

AUTHOR UNKNOWN

TAKE A LESSON

Take the lesson to thyself,
Loving heart and true;
Golden years are fleeting by,
Youth is passing, too.
Learn to make the most of life;
Lose no happy day.
Time will never bring thee back
Chances swept away.

Leave no tender word unsaid;
Love while life shall last:
"The mill will never grind
With the water that has passed."
Take the proverb to thine heart,
Take! oh hold it fast:
"The mill will never grind
With the water that has passed!"

AUTHOR UNKNOWN

Additional poems about opportunity appear in the topics "Choice and Accountability," "Life," "Success," and elsewhere.

PATRIOTISM

LORD, WHILE FOR ALL MANKIND WE PRAY

Lord, while for all mankind we pray,
Of every clime and coast,
O hear us for our native land,
The land we love the most.

O guard our shores from every foe;
With peace our borders bless;
With prosperous times our cities crown,
Our fields with plenteousness.

Unite us in the sacred love
Of knowledge, truth, and Thee,
And let our hills and valleys shout
The songs of liberty.

Lord of the nations, thus to Thee
Our country we commend;
Be Thou her refuge and her trust,
Her everlasting friend.

JOHN R. WREFORD

A FATHER'S TRIBUTE

I don't know what they'll put him at, or what his post may be;
I cannot guess the task that waits for him across the sea,
But I have known him through the years, and when there's work to
    do,
I know he'll meet his duty well, I'll swear that he'll be true.

I sometimes fear that he may die, but never that he'll shirk;
If death shall want him death must go and take him at his work;
This splendid sacrifice he makes is filled with terrors grim,
And I have many thoughts of fear, but not one fear of him.

The foe may rob my life of joy, the foe may take my all,
And desolate my days shall be if he shall have to fall,

236

But this I know, whate'er may be the grief that I must face,
Upon his record there will be no blemish of disgrace.

His days have all been splendid days, there lies no broken trust
Along the pathway of his youth to molder in the dust;
Honor and truth have marked his ways, in him I can be glad;
He is as fine and true a son as ever a father had.

EDGAR A. GUEST

FROM THE NEW COLOSSUS

Give me your tired, your poor,
Your huddled masses yearning to breathe free;
The wretched refuse of your teeming shore.
Send these, the homeless, tempest-tossed to me,
I lift my lamp beside the golden door.

EMMA LAZARUS

GOD BLESS OUR NATIVE LAND

God bless our native land;
Firm may she ever stand
    Through storm and night:
When the wild tempests rave,
Ruler of wind and wave,
Thou who art strong to save,
    Be Thou her might!

For her our prayer shall be,
Our fathers' God, to Thee,
    On whom we wait:
Be her walls, holiness,
Her rulers, righteousness,
In all her homes be peace,
    God save the State!

Not for this land alone,
But be God's mercies shown
    From shore to shore;
And may the nations see
That men should brothers be,

237

And form one family
The wide world o'er.

SIEGFRIED A. MAHLMANN
AND WILLIAM E. HICKSON

BREATHES THERE THE MAN
FROM *THE LAY OF THE LAST MINSTREL*

Breathes there the man, with soul so dead,
Who never to himself hath said,
   This is my own, my native land!
Whose heart hath ne'er within him burned,
As home his footsteps he hath turned,
   From wandering on a foreign strand?
If such there breathe, go, mark him well!
For him no minstrel raptures swell;
High though his titles, proud his name,
Boundless his wealth, as wish can claim—
Despite those titles, power and pelf,
The wretch, concentered all in self,
Living, shall forfeit fair renown,
And, doubly dying, shall go down
To the vile dust from whence he sprung,
Unwept, unhonored and unsung.

SIR WALTER SCOTT

VICTORY
(FOUND ON THE BODY OF AN AUSTRALIAN SOLDIER)

Ye that have faith to look with fearless eyes
   Beyond the tragedy of a world at strife,
And know that out of death and night shall rise
   The dawn of ampler life:
Rejoice, whatever anguish rend the heart,
   That God has given you the priceless dower
To live in these great times and have your part
   In Freedom's crowning hour,
That ye may tell your sons who see the light
   High in the heavens—their heritage to take—
"I saw the powers of darkness take their flight;
   I saw the morning break."

AUTHOR UNKNOWN

THE FLAG WITHOUT A STAIN

For years and years I've waved o'er my people,
    O'er land and sea, o'er church tower and steeple;
Foremost in battle proudly I reign,
    Triumphant now o'er thee, without one stain.
O, how I trembled when called alone to stand,
    But brave hearts sustained me to wave o'er the land.
O, my America! O, my America!
    Proudly I wave o'er thee, Sweet land of Liberty.

No flag on earth shall insult this nation,
    Justice and right shall e'er be our relation.
No creed or sect shall here ever reign.
    While floats the Stars and Stripes, without one stain.
Stars that were blotted are shining once again,
    The Angel of Peace has wiped out the stain.

AUTHOR UNKNOWN

WHAT MAKES A NATION GREAT?

Not serried ranks with flags unfurled,
Not armored ships that gird the world,
Not hoarded wealth nor busy mills,
Not cattle on a thousand hills,
Not sages wise, nor schools nor laws,
Not boasted deeds in freedom's cause—
All these may be, and yet the state
In the eye of God be far from great.

That land is great which knows the Lord,
Whose songs are guided by His word;
Where justice rules 'twixt man and man,
Where love controls in art and plan;
Where, breathing in his native air,
Each soul finds joy in praise and prayer—
Thus may our country, good and great,
Be God's delight—man's best estate.

ALEXANDER BLACKBURN

*Additional poems about patriotism appear in the topics "Courage," "Peace,"
"Thanksgiving," and elsewhere.*

PEACE

PRAYER FOR PEACE

O God, whose will is life and peace
    For all the sons of men,
Let not our human hates release
    The sword's dread power again.
Forgive our narrowness of mind;
    Destroy false pride, we plead:
Deliver us and all mankind
    From selfishness and greed.

O God, whose ways shall lead to peace,
    Enlighten us, we pray;
Dispel our darkness and increase
    The light along our way.
Illumine those who lead the lands
    That they may make at length
The laws of right to guide the hands
    That wield the nations' strength.

O God, who callest us to peace,
    We join with everyone
Who does his part that wars may cease
    And justice may be done.
Enable us to take the way
    The Prince of Peace hath trod;
Create the will to build each day
    The family of God.

ROLLAND W. SCHLOERB

COME UNTO HIM

I wander through the still of night,
When solitude is ev'rywhere—
Alone, beneath the starry light,
And yet I know that God is there.

I kneel upon the grass and pray;
An answer comes without a voice.
It takes my burden all away
And makes my aching heart rejoice.

When I am filled with strong desire
And ask a boon of him, I see
No miracle of living fire,
But what I ask flows into me.

And when the tempest rages high
I feel no arm around me thrust,
But ev'ry storm goes rolling by
When I repose in him my trust.

It matters not what may befall,
What threat'ning hand hangs over me;
He is my rampart through it all,
My refuge from mine enemy.

Come unto him all ye depressed,
Ye erring souls whose eyes are dim,
Ye weary ones who long for rest.
Come unto him! Come unto him!

THEODORE E. CURTIS

DROP THY STILL DEWS

Drop thy still dews of quietness till all our striving cease;
    Take from our souls the strain and stress,
    And let our ordered lives confess
The beauty of thy Peace.

JOHN GREENLEAF WHITTIER

COME, YE DISCONSOLATE

Come, ye disconsolate, where'er ye languish;
Come to the mercy seat, fervently kneel.
Here bring your wounded hearts; here tell your anguish.
Earth has no sorrow that heav'n cannot heal.

241

Joy of the desolate, Light of the straying,
Hope of the penitent, fadeless and pure!
Here speaks the Comforter, tenderly saying,
"Earth has no sorrow that heav'n cannot cure."

Here see the Bread of Life; see waters flowing
Forth from the throne of God, pure from above.
Come to the feast of love; come, ever knowing
Earth has no sorrow but heav'n can remove.

THOMAS MOORE
THIRD STANZA, THOMAS HASTINGS

MAKE MY MORTAL DREAMS COME TRUE

Make my mortal dreams come true,
　　With the work I fain would do;
Clothe with life the weak intent,
　　Let me be the thing I meant;
Let me find in Thy employ,
　　Peace that dearer is than joy.

JOHN GREENLEAF WHITTIER

THE STORM OF LIFE

As the bird trims to the gale,
I trim myself to the storm of time,
I man the rudder, reef the sail,
Obey the voice at eve obeyed at prime:
"Lowly faithful, banish fear,
Right onward drive unharmed;
The port, well worth the cruise, is near,
And every wave is charmed."

RALPH WALDO EMERSON

HE HEARS WITH GLADDENED HEART

He hears with gladdened heart the thunder
　　Peal, and loves the falling dew;
He knows the earth above and under—
　　Sits and is content to view.

He sits beside the dying ember,
   God for hope and man for friend,
Content to see, glad to remember,
   Expectant of a certain end.

ROBERT LOUIS STEVENSON

LET US HAVE PEACE

The earth is weary of our foolish wars.
Her hills and shores were shaped for lovely things,
Yet all our years are spent in bickerings
   Beneath the astonished stars.

April by April laden with beauty comes,
Autumn by Autumn turns our toil to gain,
But hand at sword hilt, still we start and strain
   To catch the beat of drums.

Knowledge to knowledge adding, skill to skill,
We strive for others' good as for our own—
And then, like cavemen snarling with a bone,
   We turn and rend and kill. . . .

With life so fair, and all too short a lease
Upon our special star! Nay, love and trust,
Not blood and thunder shall redeem our dust.
   Let us have peace!

NANCY BYRD TURNER

Additional poems about peace appear in the topics "Jesus Christ," "Millennial Age," "Patriotism," and elsewhere.

PERSEVERANCE

THE CHAMPION

The average runner sprints
Until the breath in him is gone;
But the champion has the iron will;
That makes him carry on.

For rest, the average runner begs,
When limp his muscles grow;
But the champion runs on leaden legs
His spirit makes him go.

The average man's complacent
When he does his best to score;
But the champion does his best
And then he does a little more.

AUTHOR UNKNOWN

GOOD TIMBER

The tree that never had to fight
For sun and sky and air and light,
But stood out in the open plain
And always got its share of rain,
Never became a forest king
But lived and died a scrubby thing.

The man who never had to toil
To gain and farm his patch of soil,
Who never had to win his share
Of sun and sky and light and air,
Never became a manly man
But lived and died as he began.

Good timber does not grow with ease,
The stronger wind, the stronger trees,
The further sky, the greater length,
The more the storm, the more the strength.

244

By sun and cold, by rain and snow,
In trees and men good timbers grow.

Where thickest lies the forest growth
We find the patriarchs of both.
And they hold counsel with the stars
Whose broken branches show the scars
Of many winds and much of strife
This is the common law of life.

DOUGLAS MALLOCH
AS QUOTED IN STERLING W. SILL,
MAKING THE MOST OF YOURSELF

BILL BROWN MADE A MILLION

Bill Brown made a million—Bill Brown! Think of that!
A boy, you remember, as poor as a rat;
He hoed for the neighbors, did jobs by the day,
But Bill made a million, or near it, they say.
You can't understand it? Well, neither could I,
And then I remembered, and now I know why:
The bell might be ringing, the dinner horn blow,
But Bill always hoed to the end of the row.

Bill worked for my father, you maybe recall;
He wasn't a wonder—not that, not at all;
He couldn't out-hoe me, or cover more ground,
Or hoe any cleaner, or beat me around.
In fact, I was better in one way that I know:
One toot from the kitchen and home I would go;
But Bill always hoed to the end of the row.

We used to get hungry out there in the corn.
When you talk about music, what equals a horn?
A horn yellin' dinner, tomatoes and beans,
And pork and potatoes and gravy and greens?
I ain't blamin' no one for quittin' on time,
To stop with the whistle, that ain't a crime.
But as for the million—well, this much I know:
That Bill always hoed to the end of the row.

AUTHOR UNKNOWN

HEAVEN IS NOT REACHED AT A SINGLE BOUND

Heaven is not reached at a single bound;
   But we build the ladder by which we rise
   From the lowly earth to the vaulted skies,
And we mount its summit round by round.

I count this thing to be grandly true:
   That a noble deed is a step toward God,
   Lifting the soul from the common clod
To a purer air and a broader view.

We rise by the things that are under feet;
   By what we have mastered of good and gain;
   By the pride deposed and the passion slain,
And the vanquished ills that we hourly meet.

We hope, we aspire, we resolve, we trust,
   When the morning calls us to life and light,
   But our hearts grow weary, and, ere the night,
Our lives are trailing the sordid dust.

We hope, we resolve, we aspire, we pray,
   And we think that we mount the air on wings
   Beyond the recall of sensual things,
While our feet still cling to the heavy clay.

Wings for the angels, but feet for men!
   We may borrow the wings to find the way—
   We may hope, and resolve, and aspire, and pray;
But our feet must rise, or we fall again.

Only in dreams is a ladder thrown
   From the weary earth to the sapphire walls;
   But the dreams depart, and the vision falls,
And the sleeper wakes on his pillow of stone.

Heaven is not reached at a single bound;
   But we build the ladder by which we rise
   From the lowly earth to the vaulted skies,
And we mount to its summit, round by round.

JOSIAH GILBERT HOLLAND

ALWAYS FINISH

If a task is once begun
Never leave it till it's done.
Be the labor great or small,
Do it well or not at all.

AUTHOR UNKNOWN

YOU

You can do as much as you think you can,
But you'll never accomplish more;
If you're afraid of yourself, young man,
There's little for you in store.

For failure comes from the inside first;
It's there if you only knew it.
And you can win, though you face the worst,
If you feel you're going to do it!

EDGAR A. GUEST

IT'S THE STEADY, CONSTANT DRIVING

It's the steady, constant driving
To the goal for which you're striving,
Not the speed with which you travel
That will make the victory sure.
It's the everlasting gaining,
Without whimper or complaining
At the burdens you are bearing,
Or the woes you must endure.

It's the holding to a purpose
And the never giving in;
It's the cutting down the distance
By the little that you win.
It's the iron will to do it
And the steady sticking to it.
So, whate'er your task, go to it
And life's purpose you will win.

AUTHOR UNKNOWN

IF

If you can keep your head when all about you
    Are losing theirs and blaming it on you,
If you can trust yourself when all men doubt you,
    But make allowance for their doubting too;
If you can wait and not be tired by waiting,
    Or being lied about, don't deal in lies,
Or being hated, don't give way to hating,
    And yet don't look too good, nor talk too wise:

If you can dream—and not make dreams your master;
    If you can think—and not make thoughts your aim;
If you can meet with Triumph and Disaster
    And treat those two impostors just the same;
If you can bear to hear the truth you've spoken
    Twisted by knaves to make a trap for fools,
Or watch the things you gave your life to, broken,
    And stoop and build 'em up with worn-out tools:

If you can make one heap of all your winnings
    And risk it on one turn of pitch-and-toss,
And lose, and start again at your beginnings
    And never breathe a word about your loss;
If you can force your heart and nerve and sinew
    To serve your turn long after they are gone,
And so hold on when there is nothing in you
    Except the Will which says to them: "Hold on!"

If you can talk with crowds and keep your virtue,
    Or walk with Kings—nor lose the common touch,
If neither foes nor loving friends can hurt you,
    If all men count with you, but none too much;
If you can fill the unforgiving minute
    With sixty seconds' worth of distance run,
Yours is the Earth and everything that's in it,
    And—which is more—you'll be a Man, my son!

RUDYARD KIPLING

IF YOU CAN SMILE

If you can smile when things go wrong
And say, "It doesn't matter,"
If you can laugh off care and woe
And trouble makes you fatter;

If you can keep a happy face
When all around are blue—
Then have your head examined, Bud,
There's something wrong with you!

For one thing I've arrived at:
There are no "ands" or "buts";
The guy that's grinning all the time
Must be completely nuts.

AUTHOR UNKNOWN

THE QUITTER

Fate handed the quitter a bump, and he dropped;
The road seemed too rough to go, so he stopped.
He thought of his hurt, and there came to his mind
The easier path he was leaving behind.
"Oh, it's all much too hard," said the quitter right then;
"I'll stop where I am and not try it again."

He sat by the road and he made up his tale
To tell when men asked why he happened to fail.
A thousand excuses flew up to his tongue,
And these on the thread of his story he strung,
But the truth of the matter he didn't admit;
He never once said, "I was frightened and quit."

Whenever the quitter sits down by the road
And drops from the struggle to lighten his load,
He can always recall to his own peace of mind
A string of excuses for falling behind;
But somehow or other he can't think of one
Good reason for battling and going right on.

Oh, when the bump comes and fate hands you a jar,
Don't baby yourself, boy, whoever you are;
Don't pity yourself and talk over your woes;
Don't think up excuses for dodging the blows.
But stick to the battle and see the thing through.
And don't be a quitter, whatever you do.

AUTHOR UNKNOWN

AN INSPIRATION

However the battle is ended,
    Though proudly the victor comes,
With fluttering flags and prancing steeds
    And echo of rolling drums,
Still truth proclaims the motto,
    In letters of living light,
No question is ever settled
    Until it is settled right.

Though the heel of the strong oppressor
    May grind the weak in the dust;
And the voices of fame with one acclaim
    May call him great and just;
Let those who applaud take warning
    And keep this motto in sight—
No question is ever settled
    Until it is settled right.

Let those who have failed take courage,
    Though the enemy seems to have won;
Though his ranks are strong, if he be in the wrong,
    The battle is not yet done;
For sure as the morning follows
    The darkest hour of the night,
No question is ever settled
    Until it is settled right.

O man, bowed down with labor,
    O woman, young, yet old;
O heart, oppressed in the toiler's breast,
    And crushed by the power of gold,

Keep on with your weary battle
   Against triumphant might;
No question is ever settled
   Until it is settled right.

                       ELLA WHEELER WILCOX

NEVER GIVE UP!

Never give up! If adversity presses,
Providence wisely has mingled the cup,
And the best counsel, in all your distresses,
Is the stout watchword of "Never give up!"

                       MARTIN F. TUPPER

YOU MAY BE WHAT YOU WILL TO BE

You may be what you will to be;
Let cowards find their false content
In that poor word *environment,*
But spirit scorns it and is free.

It conquers time; it masters space;
It cows the boastful trickster chance,
And bids the tyrant circumstance
Uncrown and fill a servant's place.

The human will—that force unseen,
The offspring of a deathless soul—
Can hew its way to any goal,
Though walls of granite intervene.

                       AUTHOR UNKNOWN

STICK TO YOUR TASK

Stick to your task till it sticks to you;
Beginners are many, but enders are few.
Honor, power, place, and praise
Will come, in time, to the one who stays.

Stick to your task till it stick to you;
Bend at it, sweat at it, smile at it too;

251

For out of the bend and the sweat and the smile
Will come life's victories, after awhile.

AUTHOR UNKNOWN

SAY NOT THE STRUGGLE NOUGHT AVAILETH

Say not the struggle nought availeth,
   The labour and the wounds are vain,
The enemy faints not, nor faileth,
   And as things have been, they remain.

If hopes were dupes, fears may be liars;
   It may be, in yon smoke concealed,
Your comrades chase e'en now the fliers,
   And, but for you, possess the field.

For while the tired waves, vainly breaking,
   Seem here no painful inch to gain,
Far back, through creeks and inlets making,
   Comes silent, flooding in, the main.

And not by eastern windows only,
   When daylight comes, comes in the light,
In front, the sun climbs slow, how slowly,
   But westward, look, the land is bright.

ARTHUR HUGH CLOUGH

QUESTION NOT

Question not, but live and labor,
Till your goal be won,
Helping every feeble neighbor,
Seeking help from none;
Life is mostly froth and bubble,
Two things stand like stone—
Kindness in another's trouble,
Courage in our own.

ADAM LINDSAY GORDON

THE OYSTER

There once was an oyster
Whose story I'll tell,
Who found that some sand
Had worked under his shell.
Just one little grain
But it gave him a pain,
For oysters have feelings
That are very plain.
Now did he berate
This working of fate,
That left him in such a
Deplorable state?
Did he curse the government,
Call for an election,
And say that the sea
Should have some protection?
No! He said to himself
As he sat on the shelf,
"Since I cannot remove it,
I think I'll improve it."
Well, years passed by,
As years always do,
Till he came to his destiny,
Oyster stew!
But the small grain of sand
That bothered him so
Was a beautiful pearl
All richly aglow.
Now this tale has a moral,
For isn't it grand,
What an oyster can do
With a small grain of sand?
And what couldn't we do
If we'd only begin
With all of the things
That get under our skin?

AUTHOR UNKNOWN

WHEN YOU WANT A THING BAD ENOUGH

When you want a thing bad enough to go out and fight for it,
To work day and night for it,
To give up your peace and your sleep and your time for it;
If only the desire of it makes your aim strong enough never to tire of it;
If life seems all empty and useless without it,
And all that you dream and you scheme is about it;
If gladly you'll sweat for it, fret for it, plan for it,
Pray with all your strength for it;
If you'll simply go after the thing that you want with all your capacity,
Strength and sagacity; faith, hope, and confidence, stern pertinacity;
If neither poverty nor cold nor famish nor gaunt
Nor sickness or pain to body or brain can turn you away
From the aim that you want;
If dogged and grim, you besiege and beset it, you'll get it!

AUTHOR UNKNOWN

*Additional poems about perseverance appear in the topics "Adversity,"
"Courage," "Success," and elsewhere.*

PRAYER AND WORSHIP

ANCHORED TO THE INFINITE

The builder who first bridged Niagara's gorge,
Before he swung his cable, shore to shore,
Sent out across the gulf his venturing kite
Bearing a slender cord for unseen hands
To grasp upon the further cliff and draw
A greater cord, and then a greater yet;
Till at the last across the chasm swung
The cable—then a mighty bridge in air!

So we may send our little timid thought
Across the void, out to God's reaching hands—
Send out our love and faith to thread the deep,
Thought after thought until the little cord
Has greatened to a chain no chance can break,
And—we are anchored to the Infinite!

EDWIN MARKHAM

TO SAY MY PRAYER

To say my prayer is not to pray,
Unless I mean the words I say,
Unless I think to whom I speak,
And with my heart his favor seek.

Then let me, when I come to pray,
Not only mean the words I say,
But let me strive with earnest care,
To have my heart go with my prayer.

AUTHOR UNKNOWN

HE PRAYETH BEST WHO LOVETH BEST

He prayeth best who loveth best
All things, both great and small;
For the dear God who loveth us,
He made and loveth all.

SAMUEL TAYLOR COLERIDGE

255

MORE THINGS ARE WROUGHT BY PRAYER

More things are wrought by prayer
Than this world dreams of. Wherefore, let thy voice
Rise like a fountain for me night and day.
For what are men better than sheep or goats
That nourish a blind life within the brain,
If, knowing God, they lift not hands of prayer
Both for themselves and those who call them friends?
For so the whole round earth is every way
Bound by gold chains about the feet of God.

ALFRED, LORD TENNYSON

THEY WHO HAVE STEEPED

They who have steeped their souls in prayer
Can ever anguish calmly bear.

LORD HOUGHTON

NO TIME FOR GOD

No time for God?
What fools we are, to clutter up
Our lives with common things
And leave without heart's gate
The Lord of life and Life itself
Our God.

No time for God?
As soon to say, no time
To eat or sleep or love or die.
Take time for God
Or you shall dwarf your soul,
And when the angel death
Comes knocking at your door,
A poor misshapen thing you'll be
To step into eternity.

NORMAN L. TROTT

TEACH US, GOOD LORD

Teach us, good Lord, to serve thee as thou deservest:
    to give and not to count the cost;
    to fight and not to heed the wounds;
    to toil and not to seek for rest;
    to labor and not to ask for any reward
    save that of knowing that we do thy will.

ST. IGNATIUS OF LOYOLA

PRAYER

I know not by what methods rare,
But this I know, God answers prayer.
I know that He has given His Word,
Which tells me prayer is always heard,
And will be answered, soon or late.
And so I pray and calmly wait.
I know not if the blessing sought
Will come in just the way I thought;
But leave my prayers with Him alone,
Whose will is wiser than my own,
Assured that He will grant my quest,
Or send some answer far more blest.

ELIZA M. HICKOK

SANCTUARY

On these white walls, this House of Prayer,
The light of heaven falls everywhere.

And as we pass its sacred gate
Three lessons glorious await:

Have faith and let your faith inspire
Your fellowmen with holy fire;

Have hope and let its presence glow
That all the power of God may know;

Have love and let it steadfast be
Like unto Christ's at Calvary.

C. FRANK STEELE

GOD IS IN HIS HOLY TEMPLE

God is in his holy temple.
Earthly thoughts, be silent now,
While with rev'rence we assemble
And before his presence bow.
He is with us, now and ever,
When we call upon his name,
Aiding ev'ry good endeavor,
Guiding ev'ry upward aim.

God is in his holy temple,
In the pure and holy mind,
In the rev'rent heart and simple,
In the soul from sin refined.
Banish then each base emotion.
Lift us up, O Lord, to thee;
Let our souls, in pure devotion,
Temples for thy worship be.

AUTHOR UNKNOWN

THOU, WHOSE UNMEASURED TEMPLE STANDS

Thou, whose unmeasured temple stands,
Built over earth and sea,
Accept the walls that human hands
Have raised, O God, to Thee.

And let the Comforter and Friend,
Thy Holy Spirit, meet
With those who here in worship bend
Before Thy mercy seat.

May they who err be guided here
To find the better way;
And they who mourn, and they who fear,
Be strengthened as they pray.

May faith grow firm, and love grow warm,
And pure devotion rise,
While round these hallowed walls the storm
Of earth-born passion dies.

WILLIAM CULLEN BRYANT

258

PRAYER IS NOT ARTFUL MONOLOGUE

Prayer is not artful monologue
Of voice uplifted from the sod;
It is Love's tender dialogue
  Between the soul and God.

JOHN RICHARD MORELAND

AWAY IN FOREIGN FIELDS

Away in foreign fields they wondered how
  Their simple words had power—
At home the Christians, two or three had met
  To pray an hour.
Yes, we are always wondering, wondering how—
  Because we do not see
Someone—perhaps unknown and far away—
  On bended knee.

AUTHOR UNKNOWN

A PRAYER OF ST. FRANCIS OF ASSISI

Lord, make me an instrument of thy peace.
Where there is hatred, let me sow love;
Where there is doubt, let me sow faith;
Where there is despair, let me sow hope;
Where there is darkness, let me sow light;
Where there is sadness, let me sow joy!
O divine Master, grant that I may not so much seek
To be consoled as to console,
To be understood as to understand,
To be loved as to love.
For it is in giving that we receive;
It is in pardoning that we are pardoned;
And it is in dying that we are born to eternal life.

ST. FRANCIS OF ASSISI,
TRANS. F. ROBERT WILSON

A CHILD'S OFFERING

The wise may bring their learning,
  The rich may bring their wealth,

259

And some may bring their greatness,
    And some bring strength and health;
We, too, would bring our treasures
    To offer to the King;
We have no wealth or learning:
    What shall we children bring?

We'll bring Him hearts that love Him;
    We'll bring Him thankful praise,
And young souls meekly striving
    To walk in holy ways:
And these shall be the treasures
    We offer to the King,
And these are gifts that even
    The poorest child may bring.

We'll bring the little duties
    We have to do each day;
We'll try our best to please Him,
    At home, at school, at play:
And better are these treasures
    To offer to our King,
Than richest gifts without them;
    Yet these a child may bring.

AUTHOR UNKNOWN

LORD, IT BELONGS NOT TO MY CARE

Lord, it belongs not to my care,
    Whether I die or live;
To love and serve Thee is my share,
    And this Thy grace must give.

If life be long I will be glad,
    That I may long obey;
If short—yet why should I be sad
    To soar to endless day?

Christ leads me through no darker rooms
    Than He went through before;
He that unto God's kingdom comes,
    Must enter by this door.

Come, Lord, when grace has made me meet
　　Thy blessèd face to see;
For if Thy work on earth be sweet,
　　What will Thy glory be!

Then I shall end my sad complaints,
　　And weary, sinful days;
And join with the triumphant saints,
　　To sing Jehovah's praise.

My knowledge of that life is small,
　　The eye of faith is dim;
But 'tis enough that Christ knows all,
　　And I shall be with Him.

RICHARD BAXTER

PRAYER

He asked for strength that he might achieve;
He was made weak that he might obey.
He asked for health that he might do greater things;
He was given infirmity that he might do better things.
He asked for riches that he might be happy;
He was given poverty that he might be wise.
He asked for power that he might have the praise of men;
He was given weakness that he might feel the need of God.
He asked for all things that he might enjoy life;
He was given life that he might enjoy all things.
He has received nothing that he asked for,
All things he hoped for;
His prayer is answered; he is most blessed.

AUTHOR UNKNOWN

BE MERCIFUL

Once ran my prayer as runs the brook
　　O'er pebbles and through sunny meads;
No pain my inmost spirit shook,
　　Words broke in shallows of small needs.

But now the shadows on me lie,
    Deep-cut the channel of the years;
And prayer is but a sobbing cry
    Through whitened lips and falling tears.

Not glibly, but with broken speech,
    O God, my God, I pray to Thee;
Enough if now I may beseech,
    Be merciful, O God, to me!

JOHN T. MCFARLAND

I SAY A PRAYER EACH MORNING

I say a prayer each morning,
So the day will turn out right,
And when the sun has disappeared,
I tell the Lord good night.

The world looks brighter in the dawn
When I pronounce a prayer,
Because it reassures me
The Lord is really there,

And that I seem to walk with him
Each hour of the day,
While I am occupied with work
Or taking time to play.

I listen to his counsel
And find my courage strong
Whenever I am weary
Or when anything goes wrong.

And when the day is over
And the moon and stars are bright,
I feel the least that I can do
Is tell the Lord good night.

AUTHOR UNKNOWN

I OFTEN SAY MY PRAYERS

I often say my prayers,
  But do I ever pray?
And do the wishes of my heart
  Go with the words I say?

I may as well kneel down
  And worship gods of stone,
As offer to the living God
  A prayer of words alone.

For words without the heart
  The Lord will never hear,
Nor will he to those lips attend
  Whose prayers are not sincere.

JOHN BURTON

A PRAYER FOUND IN CHESTER CATHEDRAL

Give me a good digestion, Lord,
  And also something to digest;
Give me a healthy body, Lord,
  With sense to keep it at its best.

Give me a healthy mind, good Lord,
  To keep the good and pure in sight;
Which, seeing sin, is not appalled,
  But finds a way to set it right.

Give me a mind that is not bored,
  That does not whimper, whine or sigh;
Don't let me worry overmuch
  About the fussy thing called "I."

Give me a sense of humor, Lord,
  Give me the grace to see a joke;
To get some happiness from life,
  And pass it on to other folk.

AUTHOR UNKNOWN

263

TWO PRAYERS

Only for these I pray,
    Pray with assurance strong:
Light to discover the way,
    Power to follow it long.

Let me have light to see,
    Light to be sure and know;
When the road is clear to me
    Willingly I go.

Let me have power to do,
    Power of the brain and nerve,
Though the task is heavy and new
    Willingly I will serve.

My prayers are lesser than three,
    Nothing I pray but two:
Let me have light to see,
    Let me have power to do.

CHARLOTTE PERKINS GILMAN

SATAN TREMBLES

Satan trembles when he sees
The least of saints upon his knees.

WILLIAM COWPER

A SABBATH WELL SPENT

A Sabbath well spent brings a week of content
And help for the cares of tomorrow.
But a Sabbath profaned, whatever the gain,
Is a sure forerunner of sorrow.

AUTHOR UNKNOWN

SWEET HOUR OF PRAYER

Sweet hour of prayer! sweet hour of prayer!
That calls me from a world of care,
And bids me at my Father's throne
Make all my wants and wishes known.
In seasons of distress and grief
My soul has often found relief,
And oft escaped the tempter's snare
By thy return, sweet hour of prayer!

Sweet hour of prayer! sweet hour of prayer!
Thy wings shall my petition bear
To Him whose truth and faithfulness
Engage the waiting soul to bless.
And since He bids me seek His face,
Believe His word, and trust His grace,
I'll cast on Him my every care,
And wait for thee, sweet hour of prayer!

W. W. WALFORD

SAFELY THROUGH ANOTHER WEEK

Safely through another week
    God has brought us on our way;
Let us now a blessing seek,
    Waiting in His courts today.
        Day of all the week the best,
        Emblem of eternal rest.

JOHN NEWTON

WHAT IS PRAYER?

Prayer is the soul's sincere desire,
    Utter'd or unexpress'd;
The motion of a hidden fire
    That trembles in the breast.

Prayer is the burden of a sigh,
    The falling of a tear,

265

The upward glancing of the eye,
    When none but God is near.

Prayer is the simplest form of speech
    That infant lips can try;
Prayer the sublimest strains that reach
    The Majesty on high.

Prayer is the contrite sinner's voice
    Returning from his ways,
While angels in their songs rejoice,
    And cry, Behold, he prays!

Prayer is the Christian's vital breath,
    The Christian's native air;
His watchword at the gates of death;
    He enters heaven with prayer.

The saints in prayer appear as one
    In word, and deed, and mind;
While with the Father and the Son
    Sweet fellowship they find.

Nor prayer is made by man alone:
    The Holy Spirit pleads;
And Jesus, on the eternal Throne,
    For mourners intercedes.

O Thou, by whom we come to God!
    The Life, the Truth, the Way!
The path of prayer Thyself hast trod:
    Lord! teach us how to pray!

JAMES MONTGOMERY

Additional poems about prayer and worship appear in the topics "God," "Gratitude," "Jesus Christ," and elsewhere.

SELF-MASTERY

YOUR TASK

"Your task, to build a better world," God said.
I answered, "How?
This world is such a large, vast place,
    So complicated now.
And I so small and useless am,
There's nothing I can do."
But God in all his wisdom said,
    "Just build a better you."

AUTHOR UNKNOWN

SELF-MASTERY

What tho I conquer my enemies,
    And lay up store and pelf,
I am a conqueror poor indeed,
    Till I subdue myself.

What tho I read and learn by heart
    Whole books while I am young,
I am a linguist in disgrace,
    Who cannot guard my tongue.

What tho on campus I excel
    A champ in meet and fight
If trained efficient still I can't
    Control an appetite.

What tho exemptions write my name
    High on the honor roll
Electives, solids fail me if
    I learn no self-control.

And tho I graduate and soar
    And life is good to me,
My heart shall write me failure till
    I learn self-mastery.

A. BERTHA KLEINMAN

IMMORTAL LIFE IS SOMETHING TO BE EARNED

Immortal life is something to be earned,
By slow, self-conquest, comradeship with pain,
And patient seeking after higher truths.
We cannot follow our own wayward wills
And feed our baser appetites and give
Loose reins to foolish tempers, year on year,
And then cry, "Lord, forgive me, I believe—"
And straightway bathe in glory. Men must learn
God's system is too great a thing for that;
The spark divine dwells in each soul, and we
Can fan it to a steady flame of light,
Whose lustre gilds the pathway of the tomb
And shines on through eternity, or else
Neglect it till it simmers down to death
And leaves us but the darkness of the grave.
Each conquered passion feeds the living flame;
Each well-borne sorrow is a step toward God.
Faith cannot rescue, and no blood redeem
The soul that will not reason and resolve.
Lean on thyself, yet prop thyself with prayer,
For these are spirits, messengers of light,
Who come at call and fortify thy strength,
Make friends with thee and with thine inner self,
Cast out all envy, bitterness, and hate,
And keep the mind's fair tabernacle pure;
Shake hands with Pain, give greeting unto Grief,
Those angels in disguise; and thy glad soul,
From light to light, from star to shining star,
Shall climb and claim blest immortality.

ELLA WHEELER WILCOX

HIGHER YET AND HIGHER

Higher yet and higher,
　Out of clouds in night,
Nearer yet and nearer,
　Rising to the light.

AUTHOR UNKNOWN

FORBEARANCE

Hast thou named all the birds without a gun?
Loved the wood-rose, and left it on its stalk?
At rich men's tables eaten bread and pulse?
Unarmed, faced danger with a heart of trust?
And loved so well a high behavior,
In man or maid, that thou from speech refrained,
Nobility more nobly to repay?
O, be my friend, and teach me to be thine!

RALPH WALDO EMERSON

SCHOOL THY FEELINGS

School thy feelings, O my brother;
Train thy warm, impulsive soul.
Do not its emotions smother,
But let wisdom's voice control.
School thy feelings; there is power
In the cool, collected mind.
Passion shatters reason's tower,
Makes the clearest vision blind.

School thy feelings; condemnation
Never pass on friend or foe,
Though the tide of accusation
Like a flood of truth may flow.
Hear defense before deciding,
And a ray of light may gleam,
Showing thee what filth is hiding
Underneath the shallow stream.

Should affliction's acrid vial
Burst o'er thy unsheltered head,
School thy feelings to the trial;
Half its bitterness hath fled.
Art thou falsely, basely, slandered?
Does the world begin to frown?
Gauge thy wrath by wisdom's standard;
Keep thy rising anger down.

269

Rest thyself on this assurance:
Time's a friend to innocence,
And the patient, calm endurance
Wins respect and aids defense.
Noblest minds have finest feelings;
Quiv'ring strings a breath can move;
And the gospel's sweet revealings
Tune them with the key of love.

Hearts so sensitively molded
Strongly fortified should be,
Trained to firmness and enfolded
In a calm tranquility.
Wound not willfully another;
Conquer haste with reason's might;
School thy feelings, sister, brother;
Train them in the path of right.

School thy feelings, O my brother;
Train thy warm, impulsive soul.
Do not its emotions smother,
But let wisdom's voice control.

CHARLES W. PENROSE

I DO NOT ASK FOR ANY CROWN

I do not ask for any crown
    But that which all may win;
Nor try to conquer any world
    Except the one within.

LOUISA MAY ALCOTT

A LITTLE EXPLAINED

A little explained,
A little endured,
A little passed over,
And the quarrel is cured.

AUTHOR UNKNOWN

NOW 'TIS THE SPRING

Now 'tis the spring, and weeds are shallow-rooted;
Suffer them now and they'll o'ergrow the garden.

WILLIAM SHAKESPEARE, *KING HENRY VI* 2.3.1.31–32

MAN-MAKING

We are all blind until we see
    That in the human plan
Nothing is worth the making if
    It does not make the man.

Why build these cities glorious
    If man unbuilded goes?
In vain we build the world, unless
    The builder also grows.

EDWIN MARKHAM

*Additional poems about self-mastery appear in the topics "Character," "Choice
and Accountability," "Perseverance," "Success," and elsewhere.*

SERVICE

SOMEBODY'S MOTHER

The woman was old and ragged and gray
   And bent with the chill of the Winter's day.
The street was wet with a recent snow,
   And the woman's feet were aged and slow.
She stood at the crossing and waited long,
   Alone, uncared for, amid the throng
Of human beings who passed her by
   Nor heeded the glance of her anxious eye.

Down the street, with laughter and shout,
   Glad in the freedom of "school let out,"
Came the boys like a flock of sheep,
   Hailing the snow piled white and deep.
One paused beside her and whispered low,
   "I'll help you cross, if you wish to go? . . .
She's somebody's mother, boys, you know,
   For all she's aged and poor and slow.

"And I hope some fellow will lend a hand
   To help my mother, you understand,
If ever she's poor and old and gray,
   When her own dear boy is far away."
And "somebody's mother" bowed low her head
   In her home that night, and the prayer she said
Was, "God be kind to the noble boy,
   Who is somebody's son, and pride and joy."

MARY DOW BRINE

REWARD OF SERVICE

The sweetest lives are those to duty wed,
Whose deeds both great and small
Are close-knit strands of an unbroken thread,
Where love ennobles all.
The world may sound no trumpets, ring no bells,
The Book of Life the slurring record tells.

Thy love shall chant its own beatitudes,
After its own like working. A child's kiss
Set on thy singing lips shall make thee glad;
A poor man served by thee shall make thee rich;
A sick man helped by thee shall make thee strong;
Thou shalt be served thyself by every sense
Of service which thou renderest.

ELIZABETH BARRETT BROWNING

REVELATION

I knelt to pray when day was done.
And prayed, "O Lord bless everyone;
Lift from each saddened heart the pain
And let the sick be well again."
And then I woke another day
And carelessly went on my way.

The whole day long I did not try
To wipe a tear from any eye;
I did not try to share the load
Of any brother on my road;
I did not even go to see
The sick man just next door to me.

Yet once again when day was done
I prayed, "O Lord, bless everyone."
But as I prayed, into my ear
There came a voice that whispered clear:
"Pause, hypocrite, before you pray,
Whom have you tried to bless today?

God's sweetest blessings always go
By hands that serve him here below."
And then I hid my face, and cried,
"Forgive me, God, for I have lied;
Let me but see another day
And I will live the way I pray."

WHITNEY MONTGOMERY

THE MAN OF SORROWS

Christ claims our help in many a strange disguise;
Now, fever-ridden, on a bed He lies;
Homeless He wanders now beneath the stars;
Now counts the number of His prison bars;
Now bends beside us, crowned with hoary hairs.
No need have we to climb the heavenly stairs,
And press our kisses on His feet and hands;
In every man that suffers, He, the Man of Sorrows, stands!

AUTHOR UNKNOWN

HOW THE GREAT GUEST CAME

Before the cathedral in grandeur rose
At Ingelburg where the Danube goes;
Before its forest of silver spires
Went airily up to the clouds and fires;
Before the oak had ready a beam,
While yet the arch was stone and dream—
There where the altar was later laid,
Conrad, the cobbler, plied his trade.

* * *

It happened one day at the year's white end—
Two neighbors called on their old-time friend;
And they found the shop, so meager and mean,
Made gay with a hundred boughs of green.
Conrad was stitching with face ashine,
But suddenly stopped as he twitched a twine:
"Old friends, good news! At dawn today,
As the cocks were scaring the night away,
The Lord appeared in a dream to me,
And said, 'I am coming your Guest to be!'
So I've been busy with feet astir,
Strewing the floor with branches of fir.
The wall is washed and the shelf is shined,
And over the rafter the holly twined.
He comes today, and the table is spread
With milk and honey and wheaten bread."

274

His friends went home; and his face grew still
As he watched for the shadow across the sill.
He lived all the moments o'er and o'er,
When the Lord should enter the lowly door—
The knock, the call, the latch pulled up,
The lighted face, the offered cup.
He would wash the feet where the spikes had been,
He would kiss the hands where the nails went in,
And then at the last would sit with Him
And break the bread as the day grew dim.

While the cobbler mused there passed his pane
A beggar drenched by the driving rain.
He called him in from the stony street
And gave him shoes for his bruisèd feet.
The beggar went and there came a crone,
Her face with wrinkles of sorrow sown.
A bundle of fagots bowed her back,
And she was spent with the wrench and rack.
He gave her his loaf and steadied her load
As she took her way on the weary road.
Then to his door came a little child,
Lost and afraid in the world so wild,
In the big, dark world. Catching it up,
He gave it the milk in the waiting cup,
And led it home to its mother's arms,
Out of the reach of the world's alarms.

The day went down in the crimson west
And with it the hope of the blessed Guest,
And Conrad sighed as the world turned gray:
"Why is it, Lord, that your feet delay?
Did You forget that this was the day?"
Then soft in the silence a Voice he heard:
"Lift up your heart, for I kept my word.
Three times I came to your friendly door;
Three times my shadow was on your floor.
I was the beggar with bruisèd feet;
I was the woman you gave to eat;
I was the child on the homeless street!"

EDWIN MARKHAM

OTHERS

Lord, let me live from day to day
   In such a self-forgetful way
That even when I kneel to pray,
   My prayers will be for others.

Help me in all the work I do
   To ever be sincere and true
And know that all I do for you
   Must needs be done for others.

Let "self" be crucified and slain
   And buried deep; and all in vain
May efforts be to rise again
   Unless to live for others.

And when my work on earth is done
   And my new work in heaven's begun,
May I forget the crown I've won
   While thinking still of others.

Others, Lord, yes, others,
   Let this my motto be;
Help me to live for others,
   That I may live like thee.

CHARLES D. MEIGS

A PLEA

God grant me these: the strength to do
   Some needed service here;
The wisdom to be brave and true;
   The gift of vision clear.
That in each task that comes to me
Some purpose I may plainly see.

God teach me to believe that I
   Am stationed at a post,
Although the humblest 'neath the sky,
   Where I am needed most.
And that, at last, if I do well
My humble services will tell.

God grant me faith to stand on guard,
  Uncheered, unspoke, alone,
And see behind such duty hard
  My service to the throne.
Whate'er my task, be this my creed:
I am on earth to fill a need.

EDGAR A. GUEST

PASS IT ON

Have you had a kindness shown?
  Pass it on.

'Twas not given for thee alone.
  Pass it on.

Let it travel down the years,
Let it wipe another's tears,
Till in heaven the deed appears.
  Pass it on.

HENRY BURTON

FROM A CREED

There is a destiny that makes us brothers;
  None goes his way alone:
All that we send into the lives of others
  Comes back into our own.

EDWIN MARKHAM

HOW SWEET 'TWILL BE AT EVENING

How sweet 'twill be at evening
If you and I can say,
Good Master, we've been seeking
The lambs that went astray.
Heartsore and faint from hunger,
We heard them making moan,
And lo, we've come at nightfall
Bringing them safely home.

AUTHOR UNKNOWN

277

I'LL GO WHERE YOU WANT ME TO GO

It may not be on the mountain height
Or over the stormy sea,
It may not be at the battle's front
My Lord will have need of me.
But if, by a still, small voice he calls
To paths that I do not know,
I'll answer, dear Lord, with my hand in thine:
I'll go where you want me to go.

Perhaps today there are loving words
Which Jesus would have me speak;
There may be now in the paths of sin
Some wand'rer whom I should seek.
O Savior, if thou wilt be my guide,
Tho dark and rugged the way,
My voice shall echo the message sweet:
I'll say what you want me to say.

There's surely somewhere a lowly place
In earth's harvest fields so wide
Where I may labor through life's short day
For Jesus, the Crucified.
So trusting my all to thy tender care,
And knowing thou lovest me,
I'll do thy will with a heart sincere:
I'll be what you want me to be.

I'll go where you want me to go, dear Lord,
Over mountain or plain or sea;
I'll say what you want me to say, dear Lord;
I'll be what you want me to be.

MARY BROWN

OBEDIENCE

I said: "Let me walk in the fields."
    He said: "No, walk in the town."
I said: "There are no flowers there."
    He said: "No flowers, but a crown."

278

I said: "But the skies are black;
   There is nothing but noise and din."
And He wept as He sent me back—
   "There is more," He said; "there is sin."

I said: "But the air is thick,
   And fogs are veiling the sun."
He answered: "Yet souls are sick,
   And souls in the dark undone!"

I said: "I shall miss the light,
   And friends will miss me, they say."
He answered: "Choose tonight
   If I am to miss you or they."

I pleaded for time to be given.
   He said: "Is it hard to decide?
It will not seem so hard in heaven
   To have followed the steps of your Guide."

I cast one look at the fields,
   Then set my face to the town;
He said, "My child, do you yield?
   Will you leave the flowers for the crown?"

Then into His hand went mine;
   And into my heart came He;
And I walk in a light divine,
   The path I had feared to see.

GEORGE MACDONALD

THE BRIDGE BUILDER

An old man going a lone highway
Came at the evening, cold and gray,
To a chasm, vast and wide and steep,
With waters rolling cold and deep.
The old man crossed in the twilight dim,
That sullen stream had no fears for him;
But he turned when safe on the other side,
And built a bridge to span the tide.

"Old man," said a fellow pilgrim near,
"You are wasting your strength with building here.
Your journey will end with the ending day,
You never again will pass this way.
You've crossed the chasm, deep and wide,
Why build you this bridge at eventide?"

The builder lifted his old gray head.
"Good friend, in the path I have come," he said,
"There followeth after me today
A youth whose feet must pass this way.
This chasm that has been naught to me
To that fair-haired youth may a pitfall be.
He, too, must cross in the twilight dim—
Good friend, I am building the bridge for him."

WILL ALLEN DROMGOOLE

MAKE THE WORLD BRIGHTER

Go gladden the lonely, the dreary;
Go comfort the weeping, the weary;
Go scatter kind deeds on your way.
Oh, make the world brighter today!

MRS. FRANK A. BRECK

I SHALL NOT PASS AGAIN THIS WAY

The bread that bringeth strength I want to give,
The water pure that bids the thirsty live;
I want to help the fainting day by day;
I'm sure I shall not pass again this way.

I want to give the oil of joy for tears,
The faith to conquer crowding doubts and fears.
Beauty for ashes may I give always;
I'm sure I shall not pass again this way.

I want to give good measure running o'er,
And into angry hearts I want to pour
The answer soft that turneth wrath away;
I'm sure I shall not pass again this way.

I want to give to others hope and faith,
I want to do all that the Master saith;
I want to live aright from day to day;
I'm sure I shall not pass again this way.

ELLEN H. UNDERWOOD

Additional poems about service appear in the topics "Friendship," "Good Works," and elsewhere.

SIN AND REPENTANCE

WHAT WIN I?

What win I, if I gain the thing I seek?
A dream, a breath, a froth of fleeting joy.
Who buys a minute's mirth to wail a week?
Or sells eternity to get a toy?
For one sweet grape who will the vine destroy?

WILLIAM SHAKESPEARE, LUCRECE

ALL THE WATER IN THE WORLD

All the water in the world,
However hard it tried,
Could never sink the smallest ship
Unless it got inside.

And all the evil in the world,
The blackest kind of sin,
Can never hurt you the least bit
Unless you let it in.

AUTHOR UNKNOWN

A FENCE OR AN AMBULANCE

'Twas a dangerous cliff, as they freely confessed,
Though to walk near its crest was so pleasant;
But over its terrible edge there had slipped
A duke and full many a peasant.
So the people said something would have to be done,
But their project did not at all tally;
Some said, "Put a fence around the edge of the cliff,"
Some, "An ambulance down in the valley."

But the cry for the ambulance carried the day,
For it spread through the neighboring city;
A fence may be useful or not, it is true,
But each heart became brimful of pity

For those who slipped over that dangerous cliff;
And the dwellers in highway and alley
Gave pounds or gave pence, not to put up a fence,
But an ambulance down in the valley.

"For the cliff is all right, if you're careful," they said,
"And, if folks even slip and are dropping,
It isn't the slipping that hurts them so much,
As the shock down below when they're stopping."
So day after day, as these mishaps occurred,
Quick forth would these rescuers sally
To pick up the victims who fell off the cliff,
With their ambulance down in the valley.

Then an old sage remarked: "It's a marvel to me
That people give far more attention
To repairing results than to stopping the cause,
When they'd much better aim at prevention.
Let us stop at its source all this mischief," cried he,
"Come, neighbors and friends, let us rally;
If the cliff we will fence we might almost dispense
With the ambulance down in the valley."

"Oh, he's a fanatic," the others rejoined,
"Dispense with the ambulance? Never!
He'd dispense with all charities, too, if he could;
No! No! We'll support them forever.
Aren't we picking up folks just as fast as they fall?
And shall this man dictate to us? Shall he?
Why should people of sense stop to put up a fence,
While the ambulance works in the valley?"

But a sensible few, who are practical too,
Will not bear with such nonsense much longer;
They believe that prevention is better than cure,
And their party will soon be the stronger.
Encourage them then, with your purse, voice, and pen,
And while other philanthropists dally,
They will scorn all pretense and put up a stout fence
On the cliff that hangs over the valley.

Better guide well the young than reclaim them when old,
For the voice of true wisdom is calling,
"To rescue the fallen is good, but 'tis best
To prevent other people from falling."
Better close up the source of temptation and crime
Than deliver from dungeon or galley;
Better put a strong fence round the top of the cliff
Than an ambulance down in the valley.

JOSEPH MALINS

THE DEVIL CAN CITE SCRIPTURE

The Devil can cite Scripture for his purpose.
An evil soul producing holy witness
Is like a villain with a smiling cheek,
A goodly apple rotten at the heart.
Oh, what a goodly outside falsehood hath!

WILLIAM SHAKESPEARE, THE MERCHANT OF VENICE 1.3.1.99–103

VICE IS A MONSTER

Vice is a monster of so frightful mien,
As, to be hated, needs but to be seen;
Yet seen too oft, familiar with her face,
We first endure, then pity, then embrace.

ALEXANDER POPE

WITH THOUGHTLESS AND IMPATIENT HANDS

With thoughtless and impatient hands
We tangle up the plans
The Lord hath wrought.
And when we cry in pain He saith,
"Be quiet, man, while I untie the knot."

AUTHOR UNKNOWN

DROP, DROP, SLOW TEARS

Drop, drop, slow tears,
    And bathe those beauteous feet

Which brought from heaven
    The news and prince of peace!
Cease not, wet eyes,
    His mercies to entreat;
To cry for vengeance
    Sin doth never cease;
In your deep floods
    Drown all my faults and fears;
Nor let his eye
    See sin but through my tears.

PHINEAS FLETCHER

FROM THE WORLD IS TOO MUCH WITH US

The world is too much with us; late and soon,
Getting and spending, we lay waste our powers:
Little we see in Nature that is ours;
We have given our hearts away, a sordid boon!

WILLIAM WORDSWORTH

WHEN I PUT ON MY WORN-OUT TWEEDS

When I put on my worn-out tweeds
And with my hands pull garden weeds,
The likeness always comes to mind,
'Tween weeds and sins of human kind.

For weeds will grow up anywhere
In ground that's either foul or fair,
And when you pull them, you're not through;
They'll grow right up again for you.

Some weeds have roots so great in length
That pulling them is a test of strength,
And they should be removed with care
Or they'll kill good plants anywhere.

It makes no difference where you go
There's no place that the weeds can't grow;
Some folks keep weeding, others won't,
Some folks have gardens, others don't.

So weeds and sin are quite the same
In growth and action, not in name;
But different is their origin:
God makes the weeds, we make the sin.

AUTHOR UNKNOWN

MEN TAKE THE PURE IDEALS

Men take the pure ideals of their souls
    And lock them fast away,
And never dream that things so beautiful
    Are fit for every day!
So counterfeits pass current in their lives,
    And stones they use for bread,
And starvingly and fearfully they walk
    Through life among the dead,
Though never yet was pure ideal
    Too fair for them to make their Real.

AUTHOR UNKNOWN

FOR EACH DESCENT

For each descent from fair truth's lofty way,
For each gross error which delays the soul,
By that soul's gloom and loneliness we pay,
And by the retarded journey to its goal.

AUTHOR UNKNOWN

Additional poems about sin and repentance appear in the topics "Choice and Accountability," "Forgiveness," "Jesus Christ," "Self-Mastery," and elsewhere.

SUCCESS

THE MAN WHO THINKS HE CAN

If you think you are beaten, you are;
If you think you dare not, you don't.
If you like to win, but think you can't,
It's almost a cinch you won't.
If you think you'll lose, you're lost,
For out in the world we find
Success begins with a fellow's will;
It's all in the state of mind.

If you think you're outclassed, you are;
You've got to think high to rise.
You've got to be sure of yourself before
You can ever win a prize.
Life's battles don't always go
To the stronger or faster man;
But soon or late the man who wins
Is the man who thinks he can.

WALTER D. WINTLE

DON'T QUIT

When things go wrong, as they sometimes will,
When the road you're treading seems all uphill,
When the funds are low and the debts are high,
And you want to smile, but you have to sigh,
When care is pressing you down a bit,
Rest, if you must—but don't you quit.

Life is queer with its twists and turns,
As every one of us sometimes learns,
And many a failure turns about
When he might have won had he stuck it out;
Don't give up, though the pace seems slow—
You might succeed with another blow.

287

Often the goal is nearer than
It seems to a faint and faltering man,
Often the struggler has given up
When he might have captured the victor's cup.
And he learned too late, when the night slipped down,
How close he was to the golden crown.

Success is failure turned inside out—
The silver tint of the clouds of doubt—
And you never can tell how close you are,
It may be near when it seems afar;
So stick to the fight when you're hardest hit—
It's when things seem worst that you mustn't quit.

AUTHOR UNKNOWN

SAID THE PIEMAN

The story of Simon called Simple
   Is one everybody has read;
It is sweet, it is sad, and it tells of a lad
   Who wasn't quite right in the head.
When he sought to buy pie of the pieman,
   Poor Simon was hopeful but rash,
For he childishly thought that a pie could be bought
   Without any transfer of cash.

But we mustn't speak harshly of Simon,
   Who was simply ahead of his time—
Today he could buy a whole carload of pie
   By merely investing a dime.
The up-to-date salesman would land him—
   Or, rather more likely, his wife—
By letting him pay a few cents right away
   And installments the rest of his life.

It's the way they sell pins and pianos,
   And paintings, potatoes and pants—
For a few dollars down you can buy the whole town—
   As a prospect you haven't a chance.
The fact that you're broke doesn't matter,
   Your only escape is to die—

288

And as long as they take all the money you make,
   You might as well spend it for pie!

AUTHOR UNKNOWN

GREATLY BEGIN!

Greatly begin! though thou have time
But for a line, be that sublime—
Not failure, but low aim is crime.

JAMES RUSSELL LOWELL

CAN'T

Can't is the worst word that is written or spoken
Doing more harm here than slander or lies.
   It has many a strong spirit broken,
   And with it many a good purpose dies.
It springs from the lips of the thoughtless each morning,
And robs us of courage we need through the day:
   It rings in our ears like a timely sent warning,
   And leaves when we falter and fall by the way.

Can't is the father of feeble endeavor,
The parent of terror and half-hearted work;
   It weakens the efforts of artisans clever,
   And makes of the toiler an indolent shirk.
It poisons the soul of a man with a vision,
It stifles in infancy many a plan;
   It greets honest toiling with open derision
   And mocks at the hopes and the dreams of a man.

Can't is a word that none should speak without blushing;
To utter it should be a symbol of shame;
   Ambition and courage it daily is crushing;
   It blights a man's purpose and shatters his aim.
Despise it with all of your hatred of error,
Refuse it the lodgment it seeks in your brain;
   Arm against it as a creature of terror,
   And all that you dream of you some day shall gain.

Can't is a word that is doom to ambition,
An enemy ambushed to shatter your will;
   Its prey is forever the man with a mission,
   And bows but to courage, and patience, and skill.
Hate it with hatred that is deep and undying,
For once it is welcomed 'twill break any man;
   Whatever the goal you are seeking, keep trying,
   And answer this demon by saying "I can."

EDGAR A. GUEST

THERE IS NO THING WE CANNOT OVERCOME

There is no thing we cannot overcome;
Say not thy evil instinct is inherited,
Or that some trait unborn makes thy life forlorn;
Back of thy parents and grandparents lies
The great Eternal Will!
That, too, is thine inheritance:—
Strong—beautiful—divine,
Some Lever of Success for one who tries.

AUTHOR UNKNOWN

MY WAGE

I bargained with Life for a penny,
   And Life would pay no more,
However I begged at evening
   When I counted my scanty store;

For Life is a just employer,
   He gives you what you ask,
But once you have set the wages,
   Why, you must bear the task.

I worked for a menial's hire,
   Only to learn, dismayed,
That any wage I had asked of Life,
   Life would have paid.

JESSIE B. RITTENHOUSE

NINETY AND NINE

Ninety and nine are with dreams content;
But the hope of a world made new
Is the hundredth man who is grimly bent
On making the dream come true.

TED OLSEN

WHAT IS SUCCESS?

It's doing your work the best you can,
And being just to your fellow man;
It's making money, but holding friends,
And staying true to your aims and ends;
It's figuring how and learning why,
And looking forward and thinking high,
And dreaming a little and doing much;
It's keeping always in closest touch
With what is finest in word and deed;
It's being thorough, yet making speed,
It's daring blithely the field of chance
While making labor a brave romance.
It's going onward despite defeat,
And fighting staunchly, but keeping sweet;
It's being clean and it's playing fair;
It's laughing lightly at Dame Despair;
It's looking up to the stars above,
And thinking deeply of life and love;
It's struggling on with the will to win
But taking loss with a cheerful grin;
It's sharing sorrow, and work, and mirth
And making better this good old earth;
It's serving, striving, through stain and stress;
It's doing your noblest—that's success.

AUTHOR UNKNOWN

*Additional poems about success appear in the topics "Character,"
"Opportunity," "Perseverance," and elsewhere.*

291

TEACHING

I TOOK A PIECE OF PLASTIC CLAY

I took a piece of plastic clay
    And idly fashioned it one day—
And as my fingers pressed it, still
    It moved and yielded to my will.

I came again when days were past;
    The bit of clay was hard at last.
The form I gave it, still it bore,
    And I could change that form no more!

I took a piece of living clay,
    And gently fashioned it day by day,
And molded with my power and art
    A young child's soft and yielding heart.

I came again when years were gone:
    It was a man I looked upon.
He still that early impress bore,
    And I could fashion it never more.

AUTHOR UNKNOWN

THE ECHO

'Twas a sheep not a lamb
That strayed away in the parable Jesus told,
A grown-up sheep that strayed away
From the ninety and nine in the fold.
And why for the sheep should we seek
And earnestly hope and pray?
Because there is danger when sheep go wrong:
They lead the lambs astray.
Lambs will follow the sheep, you know,
Wherever the sheep may stray.
When sheep go wrong,
It won't take long till the lambs are as wrong as they.

And so with the sheep we earnestly plead
For the sake of the lambs today,
For when the sheep are lost
What a terrible cost
The lambs will have to pay.

C. C. MILLER

MY CHUM

He stood at the crossroads all alone,
The sunlight in his face.
He had no thought for the world unknown—
He was set for a manly race.
But the roads stretched east and the roads stretched west,
And the lad knew not which road was best,
So he chose the road that led him down,
And he lost the race and the victor's crown.
He was caught at last in an angry snare
Because no one stood at the crossroads there
To show him the better road.

Another day at the self-same place,
A boy with high hopes stood.
He, too, was set for a manly race;
He, too, was seeking the things that were good.
But one was there who the roads did know.
And that one showed him which way to go.
So he turned from the road that would lead him down,
And he won the race and the victor's crown.
He walks today the highway fair
Because one stood at the crossroads there
To show him the better way.

AUTHOR UNKNOWN

HAPPY IS HE WHO WALKS THE PATH OF PEACE

Happy is he who walks the path of peace,
    With faith to guide his steps day after day;
But happier, his earthly joys increase,
    Who leads another in the perfect way.

HERBERT HERSHEY

293

IF WE WORK UPON MARBLE

If we work upon marble it will perish;
If we work upon brass time will efface it;
If we work upon immortal souls,
If we imbue them with principles,
With the just fear of the Creator and love of fellowmen,
We engrave on those tablets something which will brighten all
    eternity.

DANIEL WEBSTER

THE TEACHER

Lord, who am I to teach the way
To little children day by day,
So prone myself to go astray?

I teach them knowledge, but I know
How faint they flicker and how low
The candles of my knowledge grow.

I teach them power to will and do,
But only now to learn anew
My own great weakness through and through.

I teach them love for all mankind
And all God's creatures, but I find
My love comes lagging far behind.

Lord, if their guide I still must be,
Oh, let the little children see
The teacher leaning hard on Thee.

LESLIE PINCKNEY HILL

A DIAMOND IN THE ROUGH

A diamond in the rough is a diamond, sure enough,
And before it ever sparkled it was made of diamond stuff.
But someone had to find it or it never would be found,
And someone had to grind it or it never would be ground.
But it's found, and when it's ground,

294

And when it's burnished bright,
That diamond's everlastingly giving out its light.

O teachers of our young folk,
Don't say you've done enough;
It may be that your rudest is
A diamond in the rough.

AUTHOR UNKNOWN

FINDING GOD

I helped a little child to see
That God had made a willow tree
And God became more real to me.

I tried to lead a child through play
To grow more Christlike every day,
And I myself became that way.

I joined a junior child in prayer
And as we bowed in worship there
I felt the dear Lord's loving care.

Lord, keep us ever quick to see
By guiding children we find thee.

AUTHOR UNKNOWN

I SAW TOMORROW PASSING

I saw tomorrow passing on little children's feet
And on their forms and faces her prophecies complete.
And then I saw tomorrow look at me through little children's eyes.
And I thought how carefully I must teach if I am wise!

AUTHOR UNKNOWN

Additional poems about teaching appear in the topics "Children," "Example," "Home and Family," and elsewhere.

THANKSGIVING

OVER THE RIVER AND THROUGH THE WOODS

Over the river and through the woods,
To grandmother's house we go;
The horse knows the way
To carry the sleigh,
Through the white and drifted snow.

Over the river and through the woods,
Oh, how the wind doth blow!
It stings the toes
And bites the nose
As over the ground we go.

Over the river and through the woods,
Now grandmother's house I spy!
Hurrah for the fun! Is the pudding done?
Hurrah for the pumpkin pie!

AUTHOR UNKNOWN

THE PILGRIM FATHERS

O God, beneath Thy guiding hand
    Our exiled fathers crossed the sea;
And when they trod the wintry strand,
    With prayer and psalm they worshipped Thee.

Thou heard'st, well pleased, the song, the prayer:
    Thy blessing came; and still its power
Shall onward through all ages bear
    The memory of that holy hour.

Laws, freedom, truth, and faith in God
    Came with those exiles o'er the waves,
And where their pilgrim feet have trod,
    The God they trusted guards their graves.

And here Thy name, O, God of love,
    Their children's children shall adore,

Till these eternal hills remove,
   And spring adorns the earth no more.

LEONARD BACON

LANDING OF THE PILGRIM FATHERS

The breaking waves dashed high
   On a stern and rockbound coast,
And the woods against a stormy sky
   Their giant branches tossed;

And the heavy night hung dark
   The hills and waters o'er,
When a band of exiles moored their bark
   On the wild New England shore.

Not as the conqueror comes,
   They, the truehearted, came;
Not with roll of stirring drums,
   And the trumpet that sings of fame;

Not as the flying come,
   In silence and in fear—
They shook the depths of the desert's gloom
   With their hymns of lofty cheer. . . .

What sought they thus afar?
   Bright jewels of the mine?
The wealth of seas? the spoils of war?
   They sought a faith's pure shrine!

Aye, call it holy ground,
   The soil where first they trod:
They have left unstained what there they found—
   Freedom to worship God!

FELICIA D. HEMANS

HEARTHSIDE SEASON

Loud in the night the ripe nuts fall,
Crackling like frost in heavy beams:

And bolder sounds the coyote's call
To trouble the watch-dog's close-curled dreams.
High on the garden's grape-vined wall
A predatory green eye gleams.
This is the time of the heaping bin,
Of the granary's wealth and the cellar's store,
The season for locking the firelight in
And letting the winter storm wind roar.
These are the days of tales to spin
In happy talk round the fire once more.

FRANCES HALL

GREAT KING OF HEAVEN

Great King of heav'n, our hearts we raise
To thee in prayer, to thee in praise.
The vales exult, the hills acclaim,
And all thy works revere thy name.

O Israel's God! Thine arm is strong.
To thee all earth and skies belong,
And with one voice in one glad chord,
With myriad echoes, praise the Lord.

CARRIE STOCKDALE THOMAS

Additional poems appropriate for the Thanksgiving holiday appear in the topics "God," "Gratitude," "Prayer and Worship," and elsewhere.

TRUTH

MAGNA EST VERITAS

Here, in this little Bay,
Full of tumultuous life and great repose,
Where, twice a day,
The purposeless, glad ocean comes and goes,
Under high cliffs, and far from the huge town,
I sit me down.
For want of me the world's course will not fail:
When all its work is done, the lie shall rot;
The truth is great, and shall prevail,
When none cares whether it prevail or not.

COVENTRY PATMORE

HAMMER AND ANVIL

Look forth and tell me what they do
On Life's broad field. Oh still they fight,
The false forever with the true,
The wrong forever with the right.
And still God's faithful ones, as men
Who hold a fortress strong and high,
Cry out in confidence again,
And find a comfort in the cry:
"Hammer away, ye hostile hands,
Your hammers break, God's anvil stands."

Older than pyramids or sphinx,
Old as the stars themselves, the word
Whereby, when other courage sinks,
The courage born of Heaven is stirred.
For, when God made the world and knew
That good and evil could not blend,
He planned, however men might do,
What should be, would be in the end,
And, though as thick as ocean sands
They rain the blows, the anvil stands.

* * *

Thou knowest that thy cause is just?
Then rest in that; thy cause is sure.
Thy word is true; oh, then it must
In spite of slanderous tongues endure.
As toward the crag the billow rides,
Then falls back, shattered, to its place;
As fans the breeze, the mountain sides,
Nor moves the mountain from its base—
So, in all times and in all lands
Men's hammers break. God's anvil stands.

SAMUEL VALENTINE COLE

OH SAY, WHAT IS TRUTH?

Oh say, what is truth? 'Tis the fairest gem
That the riches of worlds can produce,
And priceless the value of truth will be when
The proud monarch's costliest diadem
Is counted but dross and refuse.

Yes, say, what is truth? 'Tis the brightest prize
To which mortals or Gods can aspire.
Go search in the depths where it glittering lies,
Or ascend in pursuit to the loftiest skies:
'Tis an aim for the noblest desire.

The sceptre may fall from the despot's grasp
When with winds of stern justice he copes.
But the pillar of truth will endure to the last,
And its firm-rooted bulwarks outstand the rude blast
And the wreck of the fell tyrant's hopes.

Then say, what is truth? 'Tis the last and the first,
For the limits of time it steps o'er.
Tho the heavens depart and the earth's fountains burst,
Truth, the sum of existence, will weather the worst,
Eternal, unchanged, evermore.

JOHN JAQUES

TRUTH FOREVER ON THE SCAFFOLD

Truth forever on the scaffold;
Wrong forever on the throne;
Yet the scaffold sways the future
And beyond the dim unknown,
Standeth God among the shadows
Keeping watch above his own.

JAMES RUSSELL LOWELL

TRUTH HAS SUCH A FACE

Truth has such a face and such a mien,
As to be lov'd needs only to be seen.

JOHN DRYDEN

FROM THE COWARDICE

From the cowardice that shrinks from new truth,
From the laziness that is content with half-truth,
From the arrogance that thinks it knows all truth,
O God of truth, deliver us.

AUTHOR UNKNOWN

IT FORTIFIES MY SOUL TO KNOW

It fortifies my soul to know
That though I perish, Truth is so;
That howso'er I stray and range,
Whate'er I do, Thou dost not change.
I steadier step when I recall
That if I slip, Thou dost not fall.

ARTHUR HUGH CLOUGH

Additional poems about truth appear in the topics "God," "Integrity," "Knowledge and Wisdom," and elsewhere.

301

WORK

THAT IS YOUR PLACE

Just where you stand in the conflict, that is your place;
Just where you think that you are useless, hide not your face;
God placed you there for a purpose, whate'er it be;
Think He has chosen you for it; work loyally.

AUTHOR UNKNOWN

DUTY

I slept and dreamed that life was Beauty:
I woke and found that life was Duty:
Was then thy dream a shadowy lie?
Toil on, sad heart, courageously,
And thou shalt find thy dream to be
A noonday light and truth to thee.

ELLEN S. HOOPER

LIFTING AND LEANING

There are two kinds of people on earth today,
Just two kinds of people, no more, I say.

Not the good and the bad, for 'tis well understood
The good are half bad and the bad are half good.

Not the happy and sad, for the swift-flying years
Bring each man his laughter and each man his tears.

Not the rich and the poor, for to count a man's wealth
You must first know the state of his conscience and health.

Not the humble and proud, for in life's busy span
Who puts on vain airs is not counted a man.

No! the two kinds of people on earth I mean
Are the people who lift and the people who lean.

Wherever you go you will find the world's masses
Are ever divided in just these two classes.

And, strangely enough, you will find, too, I ween,
There is only one lifter to twenty who lean.

In which class are you? Are you easing the load
Of overtaxed lifters who toil down the road?

Or are you a leaner who lets others bear
Your portion of worry and labor and care?

ELLA WHEELER WILCOX

HORSE SENSE

A horse can't pull while kicking.
This fact I merely mention.
And he can't kick while pulling,
Which is my chief contention.

Let's imitate the good old horse
And lead a life that's fitting;
Just pull an honest load, and then
There'll be no time for kicking.

AUTHOR UNKNOWN

AS A MAN SOWETH

We must not hope to be mowers,
And to gather the ripe gold ears,
Unless we have first been sowers
And watered the furrows with tears.
It is not just as we take it,
This mystical world of ours,
Life's field will yield as we make it
A harvest of thorns or of flowers.

JOHANN WOLFGANG VON GOETHE

DO THY WORK

Do thy work, it shall succeed
   In thine or another's day;
And if denied the victor's mead,
   Thou shalt not lack the toiler's pay.

JOHN GREENLEAF WHITTIER

IT COULDN'T BE DONE

Somebody said that it couldn't be done,
But he with a chuckle replied
That "maybe it couldn't," but he would be one
Who wouldn't say so till he'd tried.
So he buckled right in with the trace of a grin
On his face. If he worried he hid it.
He started to sing as he tackled the thing
That couldn't be done, and he did it.

Somebody scoffed: "Oh, you'll never do that;
At least no one ever has done it";
But he took off his coat and he took off his hat,
And the first thing we knew he'd begun it.
With a lift of his chin and a bit of a grin,
Without any doubting or quiddit,
He started to sing as he tackled the thing
That couldn't be done, and he did it!

There are thousands to tell you it cannot be done.
There are thousands to prophesy failure;
There are thousands to point out to you, one by one,
The dangers that wait to assail you.
But just buckle in with a bit of a grin,
Just take off your coat and go to it;
Just start to sing as you tackle the thing
That "cannot be done," and you'll do it.

EDGAR A. GUEST

THE MAN THAT WANTS A GARDEN FAIR

The man that wants a garden fair,
One small or very big,
With flowers growing here and there,
Must bend his back and dig.
The things are very few in life,
That wishes can attain.
Whatever we want of any worth
We've got to work to gain.
It matters not what goal we seek,
Its secret here reposes,
We've got to work from week to week,
To get results or roses.

AUTHOR UNKNOWN

FROM THE THREE BEST THINGS

Let me but do my work from day to day,
In field or forest, at the desk or loom;
In roaring market place or tranquil room;
Let me but find it in my heart to say,
When vagrant wishes beckon me astray,
"This is my work; my blessing, not my doom.
Of all who live, I am the one by whom
This work can best be done in the right way."
Then shall I see it not too great nor small,
To suit my spirit and to prove my powers;
Then shall I cheerful greet the laboring hours,
And cheerful turn when the long shadows fall
At eventide, to play and love and rest,
Because I know for me my work is best.

HENRY VAN DYKE

THE MAN WHO DOES HIS BEST

A man must earn his hour of peace,
Must pay for it, with hours of strife and care,
Must win by toil the evening's sweet release,
The rest that may be portioned for his share.
The idler never knows it, never can.

305

Peace is the glory of the happy man,
And man must win contentment for his soul,
Must battle for it bravely day by day.
The peace he seeks is not a nearby goal.
To claim it he must tread a rugged way.
The shirker never knows a tranquil peace,
Peace but rewards the man who does his best.

AUTHOR UNKNOWN

TRUE NOBILITY

Who does his task from day to day
And meets whatever comes his way,
Believing God has willed it so,
Has found real greatness here below.

Who guards his post, no matter where,
Believing God must need him there,
Although but lowly toil it be,
Has risen to nobility.

For great and low there's but one test;
'Tis that each man shall do his best.
Who works with all the strength he can
Shall never die in debt to man.

EDGAR A. GUEST

WHO AM I?

I am the foundation of all prosperity.
I am that from which all blessings flow.
Everything that is of value in this world springs from me.
I am the salt that gives life its savor.
I am the sole support of the poor.
And the rich who think they can do without me
    live futile lives—fill premature graves.
I have made America.
I have built her matchless industries, laid her incomparable railroads,
    created her citizens, and reared her skyscrapers.

I am the friend of every worthy youth.
　If he makes my acquaintance when he is young and keeps me by
　his side throughout his life, I can do more for him than the richest
　parent.
I keep bodies clean and fit, minds alert;
　and when neglected, both bodies and minds grow fat and sluggish.
I am even the parent of genius itself.
I am represented by every paper that flies from the press,
　in every loaf of bread that springs from the oven,
　in every train that crosses the continent,
　and in every ship that steams the ocean.
Fools hate me; wise men love me.
The man who keeps his hand in mine through life
　never dies—because that which he has created with my help lives
　on after he is gone.
The man who shirks me and scorns my aid never lives—
　Never really lives, even though he may continue to breathe.
Who am I? What am I?
I am Work!

AUTHOR UNKNOWN

FROM THE LADDER OF ST. AUGUSTINE

The heights by great men reached and kept
Were not attained by sudden flight,
But they, while their companions slept,
Were toiling upward in the night.

HENRY WADSWORTH LONGFELLOW

*Additional poems about work appear in the topics "Character," "Good Works,"
"Perseverance," "Success," and elsewhere.*

INDEX OF AUTHORS

INDEX OF TITLES

313

INDEX OF FIRST LINES